The ESSENF United States History

America since 1941:
Emergence as a World Power

Gary Land, Ph.D.
Professor and Chair, Department of History
Andrews University
Berrien Springs, MI

Research & Education Association
Visit our website at
www.rea.com

Research & Education Association
61 Ethel Road West
Piscataway, New Jersey 08854
E-mail: info@rea.com

THE ESSENTIALS®
OF UNITED STATES HISTORY
America since 1941
Emergence as a World Power

Printed in the United States of America

Library of Congress Control Number 2005933132

International Standard Book Number 0-87891-717-9

What REA's Essentials® of History Will Do for You

REA's *Essentials® of History* offer an approach to the study of history that is a marked departure from what has been available traditionally. Our books are designed to steer a sensible middle course by including neither too much nor too little information.

For students, our books will help you with studying, getting through homework, writing papers, and preparing for exams. In these pocket volumes you'll find the important events and notable figures that shaped history, and the context to consider them in.

For instructors, these books can assist in reviewing or modifying course outlines. They also provide excellent material for exams and writing assignments.

REA's authors are respected experts in their fields. They present clear, well-reasoned explanations and interpretations of the complex political, social, cultural, economic and philosophical issues and developments that characterize each era.

In preparing the *Essentials® of History*, REA has made every effort to ensure their accuracy and maximize their usefulness. We believe you will find this series enjoyable and informative.

Larry B. Kling
Program Director

About the Author

Gary Land is a professor of history at Andrews University in Berrien Springs, Michigan, where he has taught in numerous capacities since 1970. He is also currently an assistant dean of the College of Arts and Sciences and chairman of the Department of History at Andrews University.

Dr. Land is a member of the American Historical Association, the Organization of American Historians, the American Studies Association, the Popular Culture Association, and the Association of Seventh-Day Adventist Historians. He is an expert in Anglo-American cultural and intellectual history, American religious history, and the history of American popular culture. He serves as an editor on many Adventist historical journals and magazines, and has written and edited numerous books and articles about the history of Adventism in America.

Contents

CHAPTER 1

WORLD WAR II, 1941 – 1945

1.1 THE ROAD TO WAR

1.1.1 *Lend-Lease*

Passed by Congress in March 1941, Lend-Lease made available $7 billion for war materials that President Franklin Roosevelt could sell, lend, lease, exchange, or transfer to any country whose defense he deemed vital to the interests of the United States. This act indicated that the U.S. was moving toward stronger support for Great Britain.

1.1.2 *Military Developments*

In April 1941, United States forces occupied Greenland; in May the president declared a state of unlimited national emergency. After Germany invaded the Soviet Union in June, the U.S. occupied Iceland the following month and made Lend-Lease available to the Soviets.

1.1.3 Atlantic Charter

Roosevelt and Winston Churchill, prime minister of Great Britain, met at sea off the coast of Newfoundland in August 1941. They signed the Atlantic Charter, calling for self-determination of peoples, equal access to raw materials, economic cooperation, freedom of the seas, and a new system of general security.

1.1.4 Merchant Ships

After the sinking of the *Reuben James,* Congress, on October 30, authorized the arming of American merchant ships and permitted them to carry cargo to Allied ports.

1.1.5 Japan

Secretary of State Cordell Hull met in the spring of 1941 with the Japanese ambassador and unsuccessfully demanded that Japan withdraw from China. In June Japan occupied Indochina; Roosevelt the next month froze Japanese assets in the United States. The following October Hideki Tojo, the war minister, became prime minister of Japan. On November 26, the United States rejected Japanese demands that it cut off aid to China.

1.1.6 Pearl Harbor

On December 7, 1941, Japanese planes attacked the U.S. naval base at Pearl Harbor in the Hawaiian Islands. They destroyed two battleships and heavily damaged six others, wrecked over 150 airplanes, and left over 2,300 servicemen dead and another 1,100 wounded.

1.1.7 Declaration of War

On December 8, Congress declared war on Japan. Three days later the Axis powers, Germany and Italy, declared war on the United States. Great Britain and the United States then established the Combined Chiefs of Staff, headquartered in Washington, to direct Anglo-American military operations.

1.1.8 Declaration of the United Nations

On January 1, 1942, representatives of 26 nations met in Washington, D.C., and signed the Declaration of the United Nations, pledging themselves to the principles of the Atlantic Charter and promising not to make a separate peace with their common enemies.

1.2 THE HOME FRONT

1.2.1 War Production Board

The WPD was established in 1942 by President Franklin D. Roosevelt for the purpose of regulating the use of raw materials.

1.2.2 Wage and Price Controls

In April 1942 the General Maximum Price Regulation Act froze prices and extended rationing. In April 1943 prices, wages, and salaries were all frozen.

1.2.3 Revenue Act of 1942

The Revenue Act of 1942 extended the income tax to the majority of the population. Payroll deduction for the income tax began in 1944.

1.2.4 Social Changes

Rural areas lost population while coastal areas increased rapidly. Women entered the work force in increasing numbers. Blacks moved from the rural South to northern and western cities with racial tensions often resulting, most notably in the June 1943 racial riot in Detroit.

1.2.5 Smith-Connolly Act

Passed in 1943, the Smith–Connolly Antistrike Act authorized government seizure of a plant or mine idled by a strike if the war effort was impeded. It expired in 1947.

1.2.6 Korematsu v. United States

In 1944 the Supreme Court upheld President Roosevelt's 1942 order that Issei (Japanese-Americans who had emigrated from Japan) and Nisei (native born Japanese-Americans) be relocated to concentration camps. The camps were closed in March 1946.

1.2.7 Smith v. Allwright

In 1944 the Supreme Court struck down the Texas primary elections, which were restricted to whites, for violating the 15th amendment.

1.2.8 Presidential Election of 1944

President Franklin D. Roosevelt, together with new Vice Presidential candidate Harry S. Truman of Missouri, defeated his Republican opponent, Governor Thomas Dewey of New York.

1.2.9 *Death of Roosevelt*

Roosevelt died on April 12, 1945, at Warm Springs, Georgia. Harry S. Truman became president.

1.3 THE NORTH AFRICAN AND EUROPEAN THEATRES

1.3.1 *January – June 1942*

Nearly 400 ships were lost in American waters of the Atlantic to German submarines.

1.3.2 *July 1942*

The United States joined in the bombing of the European continent. Bombing increased during 1943 and 1944 and lasted to the end of the war.

1.3.3 *November 1942*

The Allied army under Dwight D. Eisenhower attacked French North Africa. The French surrendered.

1.3.4 *February 1943*

In the Battle of Kassarine Pass, North Africa, the Allied army met General Erwin Rommel's Africa Korps. Although the battle is variously interpreted as a standoff or a defeat for the U.S., Rommel's forces were soon trapped by the British moving in from Egypt.

1.3.5 *May 1943*

Rommel's Africa Korps surrendered.

1.3.6 *July 1943*

Allied armies under George S. Patton invaded Sicily from Africa and gained control by mid-August.

1.3.7 *September 1943*

Moving from Sicily, the Allied armies invaded the Italian mainland. Benito Mussolini had already fallen from power and his successor, Marshal Pietro Badoglio, surrendered. The Germans, however, put up a stiff resistance with the result that Rome did not fall until June 1944.

1.3.8 *March – September 1944*

The Soviet Union began pushing into Eastern Europe.

1.3.9 *June 6, 1944*

On "D-Day," Allied armies under Dwight D. Eisenhower, now commander in chief of Supreme Headquarters, Allied Expeditionary Forces, began an invasion of Normandy, France.

1.3.10 *July 1944*

Allied armies under General Omar Bradley took the transportation hub of St. Lo, France.

1.3.11 *August 1944*

Allied armies liberated Paris. By mid-September they had arrived at the Rhine, on the edge of Germany.

1.3.12 *December 16, 1944*

At the Battle of the Bulge, the Germans counter-attacked, driving the Allies back about fifty miles into Belgium. By January the Allies were once more advancing toward Germany.

WORLD WAR II: The European and African Theatres

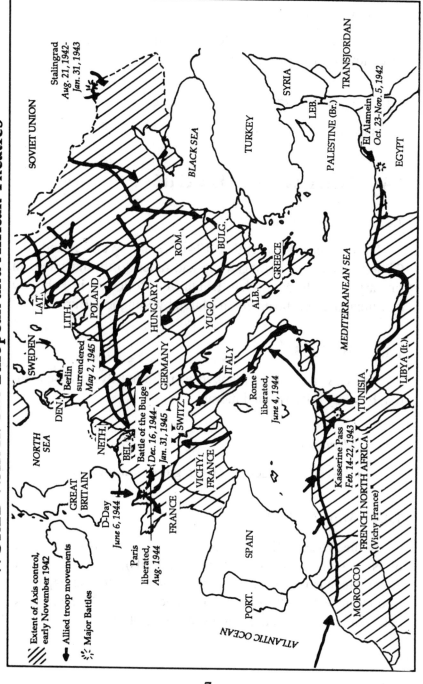

Extent of Axis control, early November 1942

Allied troop movements

Major Battles

Stalingrad Aug. 21, 1942-Jan. 31, 1943

SOVIET UNION

SWEDEN

DEN.

LAT.

LITH.

POLAND

Berlin surrendered May 2, 1945

GERMANY

HUNGARY

NETH.

BEL.

Battle of the Bulge Dec. 16, 1944-Jan. 31, 1945

SWITZ.

VICHY FRANCE

FRANCE

D-Day June 6, 1944

GREAT BRITAIN

Paris liberated, Aug. 1944

NORTH SEA

ROM.

BULG.

YUGO.

ALB.

GREECE

ITALY

Rome liberated, June 4, 1944

BLACK SEA

TURKEY

SYRIA

LEB.

PALESTINE (Br.)

TRANSJORDAN

El Alamein Oct. 23-Nov. 5, 1942

EGYPT

MEDITERRANEAN SEA

LIBYA (It.)

TUNISIA

Kasserine Pass Feb 14-22, 1943

FRENCH NORTH AFRICA (Vichy France)

MOROCCO

SPAIN

PORT.

ATLANTIC OCEAN

7

1.3.13 *March 1945*

The Allies crossed the Rhine. In the last week of April, Eisenhower's forces met the Soviet army at the Elbe.

1.3.14 *May 7, 1945*

Germany surrendered.

1.4 THE PACIFIC THEATRE

1.4.1 *The Japanese Advance*

By the end of December 1941, Guam, Wake Island, the Gilbert Islands, and Hong Kong had fallen to the Japanese. In January 1942, Raboul, New Britain fell, followed in February by Singapore and Java, and in March by Rangoon, Burma.

1.4.2 *April 1942*

The U.S. air raids on Tokyo were militarily inconsequential, but they raised Allied morale.

1.4.3 *May 6, 1942*

U.S. forces surrendered at Corregidor, Philippines.

1.4.4 *May 7 – 8, 1942*

In the Battle of the Coral Sea (northeast of Australia, south of New Guinea and the Solomon Islands), planes from the American carriers *Lexington* and *Yorktown* forced Japanese troop transports to turn back from attacking Port Moresby. The battle stopped the Japanese advance on Australia.

1.4.5 June 4 – 7, 1942

At the Battle of Midway, American air power destroyed four Japanese carriers and about 300 planes while the U.S. lost the carrier *Yorktown* and one destroyer. The battle proved to be the turning point in the Pacific.

1.4.6 August 1942 – February 1943

A series of land, sea, and air battles took place around Guadalcanal in the Solomon Islands, stopping the Japanese.

1.4.7 Island Hopping

The Allied strategy of island hopping, begun in 1943, sought to neutralize Japanese strongholds with air and sea power and then move on. General Douglas MacArthur commanded the land forces moving from New Guinea toward the Philippines, while Admiral Chester W. Nimitz directed the naval attack on important Japanese islands in the central Pacific.

1.4.8 November 1943 – June 1944

U.S. forces advanced into the Gilberts (November 1943), the Marshalls (January 1944), and the Marianas (June 1944).

1.4.9 June 19 – 20, 1944

In the Battle of the Philippine Sea, the Japanese lost three carriers, two submarines, and over 300 planes while the Americans lost 17 planes. After the American capture of the Marianas, General Tojo resigned as premier of Japan.

1.4.10 October 25, 1944

The Battle of Leyte Gulf involved three major engagements that resulted in Japan's loss of most of its remaining naval

WORLD WAR II: Far East Theatre

Legend:
- Extent of Japanese Control, Aug. 1942
- Allied Troop Movements
- Major Battles

Map labels:

SOVIET UNION

MONGOLIA

TIBET

CHINA

Manchukuo (Manchuria)

Korea

BURMA

Jan. 1944

THAILAND

FRENCH INDOCHINA

MALAYA

Sakhalin

Kuri Is.

JAPAN

Hiroshima (1st Atomic Bomb explosion) Aug. 6, 1945

Nagasaki (2nd Atomic Bomb explosion) Aug. 9, 1945

Okinawa

Iwo Jima

Mariana Is.

Guam (US)

Philippine Is. (US)

Leyte Gulf Oct. 23–26, 1944

Apr. 1945

South China Sea

Borneo

Java

DUTCH EAST INDIES

New Guinea

INDIAN OCEAN

Apr. 1944

JAPANESE MANDATE

Caroline Islands

Rabaul

Coral Sea May 7–8, 1942

Solomon Is. (Br.)

Guadalcanal

Gilbert Is. (Br.)

Ellice Is. (Br.)

Fiji Is. (Br.)

Tarawa

Marshall Is.

Eniwetok

Wake I. (US)

P A C I F I C   O C E A N

Midway *June 3–6, 1942*

Midway Is. (US)

Hawaiian Is. (US)

Pearl Harbor Dec. 7, 1941

Nov. 1943

Attu I.

Aleutian Is. (US)

Kiska I. *May 1943*

Alaska (US)

power. It also brought the first use of the Japanese kamikaze or suicide attacks by Japanese pilots who crashed into American carriers.

1.4.11 *March 1945*

Forces under General Douglas MacArthur liberated Manila.

1.4.12 *April – June 1945*

In the battle for Okinawa, nearly 50,000 American casualties resulted from the fierce fighting which virtually destroyed Japan's remaining defenses.

1.5   THE ATOMIC BOMB

1.5.1 *August 1942*

The Manhattan Engineering District was established by the Army engineers for the purpose of developing an atomic bomb (it eventually became known as the Manhattan Project). J. Robert Oppenheimer directed the design and construction of a transportable atomic bomb at Los Alamos, New Mexico.

1.5.2 *December 2, 1942*

Enrico Fermi and his colleagues at the University of Chicago produced the first atomic chain reaction.

1.5.3 *July 16, 1945*

The first atomic bomb was exploded at Alamogordo, New Mexico.

1.5.4 *August 6, 1945*

The *Enola Gay* dropped an Atomic bomb on Hiroshima,

Japan, killing about 78,000 persons and injuring 100,000 more. On August 9, a second bomb was dropped on Nagasaki, Japan.

1.5.5 *August 8, 1945*

The Soviet Union entered the war against Japan.

1.5.6 *August 14, 1945*

Japan announced its surrender. The formal surrender was signed on September 2.

1.6 DIPLOMACY

1.6.1 *Casablanca Conference*

On January 14 – 25, 1943, Franklin D. Roosevelt and Winston Churchill, prime minister of Great Britain, declared a policy of unconditional surrender for "all enemies."

1.6.2 *Moscow Conference*

In October 1943, Secretary of State Cordell Hull obtained Soviet agreement to enter the war against Japan after Germany was defeated and to participate in a world organization after the war was over.

1.6.3 *Declaration of Cairo*

Issued on December 1, 1943, after Roosevelt met with General Chiang Kai-shek in Cairo from November 22 to 26, the Declaration of Cairo called for Japan's unconditional surrender and stated that all Chinese territories occupied by Japan would be returned to China and that Korea would be free and independent.

1.6.4 Teheran Conference

The first "Big Three" (Roosevelt, Churchill, and Stalin) conference, met at Teheran from November 28 to December 1, 1943. Stalin reaffirmed the Soviet commitment to enter the war against Japan and discussed coordination of the Soviet offensive with the Allied invasion of France.

1.6.5 Yalta Conference

On February 4 – 11, 1945, the "Big Three" met to discuss post-war Europe. Stalin said that the Soviet Union would enter the Pacific war within three months after Germany surrendered and agreed to the "Declaration of Liberated Europe," which called for free elections. The Conference called for a conference on world organization, to meet in the U.S. beginning on April 25, 1945, and agreed that the Soviets would have three votes in the General Assembly and that the U.S., Great Britain, the Soviet Union, France, and China would be permanent members of the Security Council. Germany was divided into occupation zones and a coalition government of communists and non-communists was agreed to for Poland. Roosevelt accepted Soviet control of Outer Mongolia, the Kurile Islands, the southern half of Sakhalin Island, Port Arthur (Darien), and participation in the operation of the Manchurian railroads.

1.6.6 Potsdam Conference

From July 17 to August 2, 1945, Truman, Stalin, and Clement Atlee (who during the conference replaced Churchill as prime minister of Great Britain) met at Potsdam. During the conference, Truman ordered the dropping of the atomic bomb on Japan. The conference disagreed on most major issues but did establish a Council of Foreign Ministers to draft peace treaties for the Balkans. Approval was also given to the concept of war-crimes trials and the demilitarization and denazification of Germany.

CHAPTER 2

THE COLD WAR, 1945 – 1960

2.1 THE EMERGENCE OF CONTAINMENT

2.1.1 *Failure of U.S. – Soviet Cooperation*

By the end of 1945 the Soviet Union controlled most of Eastern Europe, Outer Mongolia, parts of Manchuria, Northern Korea, the Kurile Islands, and Sakhalin Island. In 1946 – 47 it took over Poland, Hungary, Rumania, and Bulgaria.

2.1.2 *Iron Curtain*

In a speech in Fulton, Missouri in 1946, Winston Churchill stated that an Iron Curtain had been spread across Europe separating the democratic from the authoritarian communist states.

2.1.3 *Containment*

In 1946, career diplomat and Soviet expert George F. Kennan warned that the Soviet Union had no intention of living peacefully with the United States. The next year, in July 1947 he wrote an anonymous article for *Foreign Affairs* in which he called for a counter-force to Soviet pressures for the purpose of "containing" communism.

2.1.4 Truman Doctrine

In February 1947 Great Britain notified the United States that it could no longer aid the Greek government in its war against communist insurgents. The next month President Harry S. Truman asked Congress for $400 million in military and economic aid for Greece and Turkey. He argued in what became known as the "Truman Doctrine" that the United States must support free peoples who were resisting communist domination.

2.1.5 Marshall Plan

Secretary of State George C. Marshall proposed in June 1947 that the United States provide economic aid to help rebuild Europe. Meeting in July, representatives of the European nations agreed on a recovery program jointly financed by the United States and the European countries. The following March, Congress passed the European Recovery Program, popularly known as the Marshall Plan, providing more than $12 billion in aid.

2.1.6 Czechoslovakia

In February 1948 the Soviets sponsored a coup d'etat in Czechoslovakia, thereby extending communism in Europe.

2.1.7 Berlin Crisis

After the United States, France, and Great Britain announced plans to create a West German Republic out of their German zones, the Soviet Union in June 1948 blocked surface

EUROPE AFTER WORLD WAR II

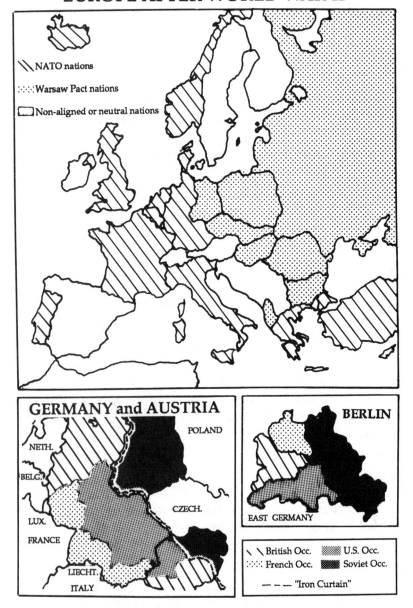

NATO nations

Warsaw Pact nations

Non-aligned or neutral nations

GERMANY and AUSTRIA

POLAND

NETH.

BELG.

CZECH.

LUX.

FRANCE

LIECHT.

ITALY

BERLIN

EAST GERMANY

British Occ. U.S. Occ.

French Occ. Soviet Occ.

— — — "Iron Curtain"

access to Berlin. The U.S. then instituted an airlift to transport supplies to the city until the Soviets lifted their blockade in May 1949.

2.1.8 *NATO*

In April 1949 the North Atlantic Treaty Organization was signed by the United States, Great Britain, France, Italy, Belgium, the Netherlands, Luxembourg, Denmark, Norway, Portugal, Iceland, and Canada. The signatories pledged that an attack against one would be considered an attack against all. Greece and Turkey joined the alliance in 1952 and West Germany in 1954. The Soviets formed the Warsaw Treaty Organization in 1955 to counteract NATO.

2.1.9 *Atomic Bomb*

The Soviet Union exploded an atomic device in September 1949.

2.2 INTERNATIONAL COOPERATION

2.2.1 *Bretton Woods, New Hampshire*

Representatives from Europe and the United States at a conference held July 1 – 22, 1944, signed agreements for an international bank and a world monetary fund to stabilize international currencies and rebuild the economies of war-torn nations.

2.2.2 *Yalta Conference*

In February 1945 Roosevelt, Churchill, and Stalin called for a conference on world organization to meet in April 1945 in the United States.

2.2.3 United Nations

From April to June 1945, representatives from fifty countries met in San Francisco to establish the United Nations. The U.N. charter created a General Assembly composed of all member nations which would act as the ultimate policy-making body. A Security Council, made up of eleven members, including the United States, Great Britain, France, the Soviet Union, and China as permanent members and six additional nations elected by the General Assembly for two-year terms, would be responsible for settling disputes among U.N. member nations.

2.3 CONTAINMENT IN ASIA

2.3.1 Japan

General Douglas MacArthur headed a four-power Allied Control Council which governed Japan, allowing it to develop economically and politically.

2.3.2 China

Between 1945 and 1948 the United States gave over $2 billion in aid to the Nationalist Chinese under Chiang Kai-shek and sent George C. Marshall to settle the conflict between Chiang's Nationalists and Mao Tse-tung's Communists. In 1949, however, Mao defeated Chiang and forced the Nationalists to flee to Formosa (Taiwan). Mao established the People's Republic of China on the mainland.

2.3.3 Korean War

On June 25, 1950, North Korea invaded South Korea. President Truman committed U.S. forces commanded by General McArthur but under United Nations auspices. By October, the U.N. (mostly American) had driven north of the 38th paral-

THE KOREAN WAR, 1950 – 1953

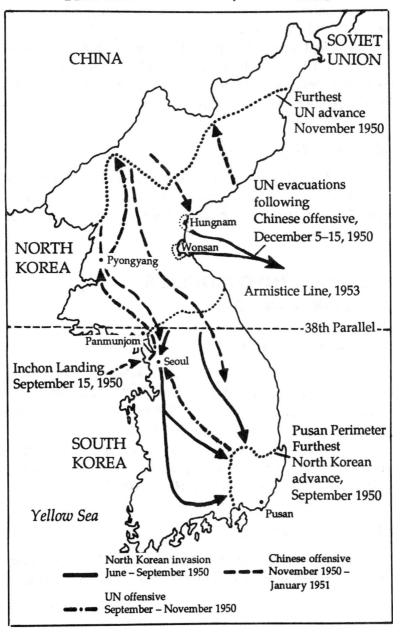

CHINA

SOVIET UNION

Furthest
UN advance
November 1950

UN evacuations
following
Chinese offensive,
December 5–15, 1950

Hungnam

Wonsan

NORTH KOREA

Pyongyang

Armistice Line, 1953

38th Parallel

Panmunjom

Inchon Landing
September 15, 1950

Seoul

Pusan Perimeter
Furthest
North Korean
advance,
September 1950

SOUTH KOREA

Yellow Sea

Pusan

North Korean invasion
June – September 1950

Chinese offensive
November 1950 –
January 1951

UN offensive
September – November 1950

19

lel, which divided North and South Korea. Chinese troops attacked MacArthur's forces on November 26, pushing them south of the 38th parallel, but by spring 1951, the U.N. forces had recovered their offensive. MacArthur called for a naval blockade of China and bombing north of the Yalu River, criticizing the president for fighting a limited war. In April 1951, Truman removed MacArthur from command.

2.3.4 *Armistice*

Armistice talks began with North Korea in the summer of 1951. In June 1953 an armistice was signed leaving Korea divided along virtually the same boundary that had existed prior to the war.

2.4   EISENHOWER-DULLES FOREIGN POLICY

2.4.1 *John Foster Dulles*

Dwight D. Eisenhower, elected president in 1952, chose John Foster Dulles as secretary of state. Dulles talked of a more aggressive foreign policy, calling for "massive retaliation" and "liberation" rather than containment. He wished to emphasize nuclear deterrents rather than conventional armed forces. Dulles served as secretary of state until ill-health forced him to resign in April 1959. Christian A. Herter took his place.

2.4.2 *Hydrogen Bomb*

The U.S. exploded its first hydrogen bomb in November 1952 while the Soviets followed with theirs in August 1953.

2.4.3   Soviet Change of Power

Josef Stalin died in March 1953. After an internal power struggle that lasted until 1955, Nikita Khrushchev emerged as the Soviet leader. He talked of both "burying" capitalism and "peaceful coexistence."

2.4.4   Asia

Vietnam. In 1954 the French asked the U.S. to commit air forces to rescue French forces at Dien Bien Phu, besieged by the nationalist forces led by Ho Chi Minh, but Eisenhower refused. In May 1954 Dien Bien Phu surrendered.

Geneva Accords. France, Great Britain, the Soviet Union, and China signed the Geneva Accords in July 1954, dividing Vietnam along the 17th parallel. The North would be under Ho Chi Minh and the South under Emperor Bao Dai. Elections were scheduled for 1956 to unify the country, but Ngo Dinh Diem overthrew Bao Dai and prevented the elections from taking place. The United States supplied economic aid to South Vietnam.

Southeast Asia Treaty Organization. Dulles attempted to establish a Southeast Asia Treaty Organization parallel to NATO but was able to obtain only the Philippine Republic, Thailand, and Pakistan as signatories in September 1954.

Quemoy and Matsu. The small islands of Quemoy and Matsu off the coast of China were occupied by the Nationalist Chinese under Chiang Kai-shek but claimed by the People's Republic of China. In 1955, after the mainland Chinese began shelling these islands, Eisenhower obtained authorization from Congress to defend Formosa (Taiwan) and related areas.

21

2.4.5 Middle East

Suez Canal Crisis. The United States had agreed to lend money to Egypt, under the leadership of Colonel Gamal Abdul Nasser, to build the Aswan Dam but refused to give arms. Nasser then drifted toward the Soviet Union and in 1956 established diplomatic relations with the People's Republic of China. In July 1956 the U.S. withdrew its loan to Egypt. In response, Nasser nationalized the Suez Canal. France, Great Britain, and Israel then attacked Egypt, but Eisenhower demanded that they pull out. On November 6 a cease fire was announced.

Eisenhower Doctrine. President Eisenhower announced in January 1957 that the U.S. was prepared to use armed force in the Middle East against communist aggression. Under this doctrine, U.S. marines entered Beirut, Lebanon in July 1958 to promote political stability during a change of governments. The Marines left in October.

2.4.6 Soviet Union

Summit Conference of 1955. In July 1955 President Eisenhower met in Geneva with Anthony Eden, prime minister of Great Britain, Edgar Faure, premier of France, and Nikita Khrushchev and Nikolai Bulganin, at the time co-leaders of the Soviet Union. They discussed disarmament and reunification of Germany but made no agreements.

Atomic Weapons Test Suspension. Eisenhower and Khrushchev voluntarily suspended in October 1958 atmospheric tests of atomic weapons.

Soviet-American Visitations. Vice President Richard M. Nixon visited the Soviet Union and Soviet Vice-Premier Anastas I. Mikoyan came to the United States in the summer of

1959. In September Premier Khrushchev toured the United States and agreed to another summit meeting.

U-2 Incident. On May 1, 1960, an American U-2 spy plane was shot down over the Soviet Union and pilot Francis Gary Powers was captured. Eisenhower ultimately took responsibility for the spy plane and Khrushchev angrily called off the Paris summit conference which was to take place in a few days.

2.4.7 Latin America

Overthrow of Guzman. The U.S. supported the overthrow of President Jacobo Arbenz Guzman of Guatemala in 1954 because he began accepting arms from the Soviet Union.

Nixon Latin American Tour. Vice President Nixon had to call off an eight-nation good-will tour of Latin America after meeting hostile mobs in Venezuela and Peru in 1958.

Cuban Revolution. In January 1959 Fidel Castro overthrew Fulgencio Batista, dictator of Cuba. Castro soon began criticizing the United States and moved closer to the Soviet Union, signing a trade agreement with the Soviets in February 1960. The United States prohibited the importation of Cuban sugar in October 1960 and broke off diplomatic relations in January 1961.

CHAPTER 3

THE POLITICS OF AFFLUENCE, 1945 – 1960

3.1 DEMOBILIZATION AND DOMESTIC POLICY

3.1.1 *Truman Becomes President*

Harry S. Truman, formerly a senator from Missouri and vice president of the United States, became president on April 12, 1945. In September 1945 he proposed a liberal legislative program, including expansion of unemployment insurance, extension of the Employment Service, a higher minimum wage, a permanent Fair Employment Practices Commission, slum clearance, low rent housing, regional TVA-type programs, and a public works program, but was unable to put it through Congress.

3.1.2 *Employment Act of 1946*

This act established a three member Council of Economic Advisors to evaluate the economy and advise the president and

24

set up a Congressional Joint Committee on the Economic Report. The act declared that the government was committed to maintaining maximum employment.

3.1.3 Atomic Energy

Congress created the Atomic Energy Commission in 1946, establishing civilian control over nuclear development and giving the president sole authority over the use of atomic weapons in warfare.

3.1.4 Price Controls

Truman vetoed a weak price control bill passed by Congress, thereby ending the wartime price control program. When prices quickly increased about 6%, Congress passed another bill in July 1946. Although Truman signed this bill, he used its powers inconsistently, especially when – bowing to pressure – he ended price controls on beef. In late 1946, he lifted controls on all items except rents, sugar, and rice.

3.1.5 Labor

In early 1946, the United Auto Workers, under Walter Reuther, struck General Motors, and steelworkers, under Philip Murray, struck U.S. Steel, demanding wage increases. Truman suggested an 18 cents-per-hour wage increase and in February allowed U.S. Steel to raise prices to cover the increase. This formula became the basis for settlements in other industries. After John L. Lewis's United Mine Workers struck in April 1946, Truman ordered the government to take over the mines and then accepted the union's demands, which included safety and health and welfare benefits. The president averted a railway strike by seizing the railroads and threatening to draft strikers into the army.

3.1.6 Demobilization

By 1947 the total armed forces had been cut to 1.5 million. The army fell to 600,000 from a WWII peak of 8 million. The Serviceman's Readjustment Act (G.I. Bill of Rights) of 1944, provided $13 billion in aid ranging from education to housing.

3.1.7 Taft-Hartley Act

The Republicans, who had gained control of Congress as a result of the 1946 elections, sought to control the power of the unions through the Taft-Hartley Act, passed in 1947. This act made the "closed-shop" illegal; labor unions could no longer force employers to hire only union members although it allowed the "union-shop" in which newly hired employees were required to join the union. It established an 80 day cooling-off period for strikers in key industries; ended the practice of employers collecting dues for unions; forbade such actions as secondary boycotts, jurisdictional strikes, featherbedding, and contributing to political campaigns; and required an anti-communist oath of union officials. The act slowed down efforts to unionize the South, and by 1954 fifteen states had passed "right to work" laws, forbidding the "union-shop."

3.1.8 Reorganization of Armed Forces

In 1947 Congress passed the National Security Act creating a National Military Establishment, National Security Council, Joint Chiefs of Staff, and Central Intelligence Agency (CIA). Together these organizations were intended to coordinate the armed forces and intelligence services.

3.1.9 Government Reorganization

Truman in 1947 appointed former President Herbert Hoover to head a Commission on Organization of the Executive Branch.

The Commission's 1949 report led to the Organization Act of 1949 which allowed the president to make organizational changes subject to congressional veto.

3.1.10 *Civil Rights*

In 1946 Truman appointed the President's Committee on Civil Rights, which a year later produced its report *To Secure These Rights.* The report called for the elimination of all aspects of segregation. In 1948 the president banned racial discrimination in federal government hiring practices and ordered desegregation of the armed forces.

3.1.11 *Presidential Succession*

The Presidential Succession Act of 1947 placed the speaker of the House and the president pro tempore of the Senate ahead of the secretary of state and after the vice president in the line of succession. The 22nd Amendment to the Constitution, ratified in 1951, limited the president to two terms.

3.1.12 *Election of 1948*

Truman was the Democratic nominee but the Democrats were split by the States' Rights Democratic Party (Dixiecrats) which nominated Governor Strom Thurmond of South Carolina and the Progressive Party which nominated former Vice-President Henry Wallace. The Republicans nominated Governor Thomas E. Dewey of New York. After traveling widely and attacking the "do-nothing Congress," Truman won a surprise victory.

3.2   THE FAIR DEAL

3.2.1   *The Fair Deal Program*

Truman sought to enlarge and extend the New Deal. He proposed increasing the minimum wage, extending Social Security to more people, maintaining rent controls, clearing slums and building public housing, and providing more money to TVA, rural electrification, and farm housing. He also introduced bills dealing with civil rights, national health insurance, federal aid to education, and repeal of the Taft-Hartley Act. A coalition of Republicans and Southern Democrats prevented little more than the maintenance of existing programs.

3.2.2   *Farm Policy*

Because of improvements in agriculture, overproduction continued to be a problem. Secretary of Agriculture Charles F. Brannan proposed a program of continued price supports for storable crops and guaranteed minimum incomes to farmers of perishable crops. It was defeated in Congress and surpluses continued to pile up.

3.3   ANTICOMMUNISM

3.3.1   *Smith Act*

The Smith Act of 1940, which made it illegal to advocate the overthrow of the government by force or to belong to an organization advocating such a position, was used by the Truman administration to jail leaders of the American Communist Party.

3.3.2   *Loyalty Review Board*

In response to criticism, particularly from the House Committee on Un-American Activities, that his administration was "soft on communism," Truman established this board in 1947 to review government employees.

3.3.3 *The Hiss Case*

In 1948 Whittaker Chambers, formerly a communist and now an editor of *Time*, charged Alger Hiss, a former State Department official and currently president of the Carnegie Endowment for International Peace, with having been a communist who supplied classified American documents to the Soviet Union. In 1950 Hiss was convicted of perjury, the statute of limitations on his alleged spying having run out.

3.3.4 *McCarran Internal Security Act*

Passed in 1950, this act required communist-front organizations to register with the attorney general and prevented their members from defense work and travel abroad. It was passed over Truman's veto.

3.3.5 *Rosenberg Case*

In 1950 Julius and Ethel Rosenberg, as well as Harry Gold, were charged with giving atomic secrets to the Soviet Union. The Rosenbergs were convicted and executed in 1953.

3.3.6 *Joseph McCarthy*

On February 9, 1950, Senator Joseph R. McCarthy of Wisconsin stated that he had a list of known communists who were working in the State Department. He later expanded his attacks to diplomats and scholars and contributed to the electoral defeat of two senators. After making charges against the army, he was censured by the Senate in 1954 and died in 1957.

3.4 EISENHOWER'S DYNAMIC CONSERVATISM

3.4.1 *1952 Election*

The Republicans nominated Dwight D. Eisenhower, most recently NATO commander, for the presidency and Richard M. Nixon, senator from California, for the vice-presidency. The Democrats nominated Governor Adlai E. Stevenson of Illinois for president. Eisenhower won by a landslide; for the first time since Reconstruction the Republicans won some Southern states.

3.4.2 *Conservatism*

Eisenhower sought to balance the budget and lower taxes but did not attempt to roll back existing social and economic legislation. Eisenhower first described his policy as "dynamic conservatism" and then as "progressive moderation." The administration abolished the Reconstruction Finance Corporation, ended wage and price controls, and reduced farm price supports. It cut the budget and in 1954 lowered tax rates for corporations and individuals with high incomes; an economic slump, however, made balancing the budget difficult.

3.4.3 *Social Legislation*

Social Security was extended in 1954 and 1956 to an additional 10 million people, including professionals, domestic and clerical workers, farm workers, and members of the armed services. In 1959 benefits were increased 7%. In 1955 the minimum wage was raised from 75 cents to $1.00 an hour.

3.4.4 *Public Power*

Opposed to the expansion of TVA, the Eisenhower administration supported a plan to have a privately owned power plant (called Dixon-Yates) built to supply electricity to Memphis, Tennessee. After two years of controversy and discovery that the government consultant would financially benefit from Dixon-Yates, the administration turned to a municipally owned power plant. The Idaho Power Company won the right to build three small dams on the Snake River rather than the federal government establishing a single large dam at Hell's Canyon. The Atomic Energy Act of 1954 allowed the construction of private nuclear power plants under Atomic Energy Commission license and oversight.

3.4.5 Farm Policy

The Rural Electrification Administration announced in 1960 that 97% of American farms had electricity. In 1954 the government began financing the export of farm surpluses in exchange for foreign currencies and later provided surpluses free to needy nations, as milk to school children, and to the poor in exchange for governmentally-issued food stamps.

3.4.6 Public Works

In 1954 Eisenhower obtained congressional approval for joint Canadian-U.S. construction of the St. Lawrence Seaway, giving ocean-going vessels access to the Great Lakes. In 1956 Congress authorized construction of the Interstate Highway System, with the federal government supplying 90% of the cost and the states 10%. The program further undermined the American railroad system.

3.4.7 Supreme Court

Eisenhower appointed Earl Warren, formerly governor of California, chief justice of the Supreme Court in 1953. That same year he appointed William J. Brennan associate justice. Although originally perceived as conservatives, both justices

31

used the court as an agency of social and political change.

3.4.8 Election of 1956

The 1956 election once again pitted Eisenhower against Stevenson. The president won handily, carrying all but seven states.

3.4.9 Space and Technology

The launching of the Soviet space satellite *Sputnik* on October 4, 1957, created fear that America was falling behind technologically. Although the U.S. launched Explorer I on January 31, 1958, the concern continued. In 1958 Congress established the National Aeronautics and Space Administration (NASA) to coordinate research and development for space exploration and the National Defense Education Act to provide grants and loans for education.

3.4.10 Sherman Adams Scandal

In 1958 the White House chief of staff resigned after it was revealed that he had received a fur coat and an oriental rug in return for helping a Boston industrialist deal with the federal bureaucracy.

3.4.11 Labor

The Landrum-Griffen Labor-Management Act of 1959 sought to control unfair union practices by establishing such rules as penalties for misuse of funds.

3.4.12 New States

On January 3, 1959, Alaska became the forty-ninth state and on August 21, 1959, Hawaii became the fiftieth.

3.5   CIVIL RIGHTS

3.5.1   *Initial Eisenhower Actions*

Eisenhower completed the formal integration of the armed forces, desegregated public services in Washington, D.C., naval yards, and veteran's hospitals, and appointed a Civil Rights Commission.

3.5.2   *Legal Background to* Brown

In *Ada Lois Sipuel v. Board of Regents* (1948) and *Sweatt v. Painter* (1950) the Supreme Court ruled that blacks must be allowed to attend integrated law schools in Oklahoma and Texas.

3.5.3   Brown v. Board of Education of Topeka

In this 1954 case, NAACP lawyer Thurgood Marshall challenged the doctrine of "separate but equal" (*Plessy v. Ferguson*, 1896). The Court declared that separate educational facilities were inherently unequal. In 1955 the Court ordered states to integrate "with all deliberate speed."

3.5.4   *Southern Reaction*

Although at first the South reacted cautiously, by 1955 there were calls for "massive resistance" and White Citizens Councils emerged to spearhead the resistance. State legislatures used a number of tactics to get around *Brown*. By the end of 1956 desegregation of the schools had advanced very little.

3.5.5   *Little Rock*

Although he did not personally support the Supreme Court decision, Eisenhower sent 10,000 National Guardsmen and 1,000 paratroopers to Little Rock, Arkansas, to control mobs and enable blacks to enroll at Central High in September 1957. A small force of soldiers was stationed at the school throughout the year.

3.5.6 Emergence of Non-Violence

On December 11, 1955, in Montgomery, Alabama, Rosa Parks, a black woman, refused to give up her seat to a white and was arrested. Under the leadership of Martin Luther King, a black pastor, blacks of Montgomery organized a bus boycott that lasted for a year, until in December 1956 the Supreme Court refused to review a lower court ruling that stated that separate but equal was no longer legal.

3.5.7 Civil Rights Acts

Eisenhower proposed the Civil Rights Act of 1957 which established a permanent Civil Rights Commission and a Civil Rights Division of the Justice Department which was empowered to prevent interference with the right to vote. The Civil Rights Act of 1960 gave the federal courts power to register black voters.

3.5.8 Ending "Massive Resistance"

In 1959 state and federal courts nullified Virginia laws which prevented state funds from going to integrated schools. This proved to be the beginning of the end for "massive resistance."

3.5.9 Sit-Ins

In February 1960 four black students staged a sit-in at a Woolworth lunch counter in Greensboro, North Carolina. This inspired sit-ins elsewhere in the South and led to the formation of the Student Nonviolent Coordinating Committee (SNCC).

3.6   THE ELECTION OF 1960

3.6.1   *The Nominations*

Vice President Richard M. Nixon won the Republican presidential nomination while the Democrats nominated Senator John F. Kennedy for the presidency with Lyndon B. Johnson, majority leader of the Senate, as his running mate.

3.6.2   *Catholicism*

Kennedy's Catholicism was a major issue until, on September 12, Kennedy told a gathering of Protestant ministers that he accepted separation of church and state and that Catholic leaders would not tell him how to act as president.

3.6.3   *Debates*

A series of televised debates between Kennedy and Nixon helped create a positive image for Kennedy and may have been a turning point in the election.

3.6.4   *Kennedy's Victory*

Kennedy won the election by slightly over 100,000 popular votes and 94 electoral votes, based on majorities in New England, the Middle Atlantic, and the South.

CHAPTER 4

SOCIETY AND CULTURE, 1945 – 1960

4.1   ECONOMIC GROWTH

4.1.1   *Gross National Product*

The GNP almost doubled between 1945 and 1960, growing at an annual rate of 3.2% from 1950 to 1960. Inflation meanwhile remained under 2% annually throughout the 1950's. Defense spending was the most important stimulant, and military-related research helped create or expand the new industries of chemicals, electronics, and aviation. The U.S. had a virtual monopoly over international trade because of the devastation of the World War. Technological innovations contributed to productivity, which jumped 35% between 1945 and 1955. After depression and war, Americans had a great desire to consume. Between 1945 and 1960 the American population grew by nearly 30%, which contributed greatly to consumer demand.

4.1.2   *Consumption Patterns*

Home ownership grew by 50% between 1945 and 1960. These new homes required such appliances as refrigerators and washing machines, but the most popular product was television, which increased from 7,000 sets in 1946 to 50 million sets in 1960. *TV Guide* became the fastest-growing magazine, and advertising found the TV medium especially powerful. Consumer credit increased 800% between 1945 and 1957 while the rate of savings dropped to about 5% of income. The number of shopping centers rose from eight in 1945 to 3,840 in 1960. Teenagers became an increasingly important consumer group, making – among other things – a major industry of rock 'n' roll music, with Elvis Presley as its first star, by the mid-1950's.

4.2 DEMOGRAPHIC TRENDS

4.2.1 *Population Growth*

In the 1950's population grew by over 28 million, 97% of which was in urban and suburban areas. The average life expectancy increased from 66 in 1955 to 71 in 1970. Dr. Benjamin Spock's *The Commonsense Book of Baby and Child Care* sold an average of one million copies a year between 1946 and 1960.

4.2.2 *The Sun Belt*

Aided by use of air conditioning, Florida, the Southwest, and California grew rapidly, with California becoming the most populous state by 1963. The Northeast, however, remained the most densely populated area.

4.2.3 *Suburbs*

The suburbs grew six times faster than the cities in the 1950's. William Levitt pioneered the mass-produced housing development when he built 10,600 houses (Levittown) on Long Island in 1947, a pattern followed widely elsewhere in the country. The Federal Housing Administration helped builders by insuring up to 95% of a loan and buyers by insuring their mortgages. Car production increased from 2 million in 1946 to 8 million in 1955, which further encouraged the development of suburbia. As blacks moved into the Northern and Midwestern cities, whites moved to the suburbs, a process dubbed "white flight." About 20% of the population moved their residence each year.

4.2.4 Middle Class

The number of American families that were classified as middle class changed from 5.7 million in 1947 to more than 12 million by the early 1960's.

4.2.5 Jobs

The number of farm workers dropped from 9 million to 5.2 million between 1940 and 1960. By 1960 more Americans held white-collar than blue-collar jobs.

4.3 CONFORMITY AND SECURITY

4.3.1 Corporate Employment

Employees tended to work for larger and larger organizations. By 1960, 38% of the workforce was employed by organizations with over 500 employees. Such environments encouraged the managerial personality and corporate cooperation rather than individualism.

4.3.2 Homogeneity

Observers found the expansion of the middle class an explanation for emphasis on conformity. David Riesman argued in *The Lonely Crowd* (1950) that Americans were moving from an inner-directed to an outer-directed orientation. William Whyte's *The Organization Man* (1956) saw corporate culture as emphasizing the group rather than the individual. Sloan Wilson's *The Man in the Grey Flannel Suit* (1955) expressed similar concerns in fictional form.

4.3.3 Leisure

The standard work week shrank from 6 to 5 days. Television became the dominant cultural medium, with over 530 stations by 1961. Books, especially as paperbacks, increased in sales annually.

4.3.4 Women

A cult of feminine domesticity re-emerged after World War II. Marynia Farnham and Ferdinand Lundberg published *Modern Woman: The Lost Sex* in 1947, suggesting that science supported the idea that women could only find fulfillment in domesticity. Countless magazine articles also promoted the concept that a woman's place was in the home.

4.3.5 Religion

From 1940, when less than half the population belonged to a church, membership rose to over 65% by 1960. Catholic Bishop Fulton J. Sheen had a popular weekly television show, "Life Worth Living," while Baptist evangelist Billy Graham held huge crusades. Norman Vincent Peale best represented the tendency of religion to emphasize reassurance with his bestseller *The Power of Positive Thinking* (1952). Critics noted the shallowness of this religion. Will Herberg in *Protestant-Catholic-Jew* (1955) said that popular religiosity lacked conviction and commitment. Reinhold Niebuhr, the leading neo-orthodox theologian, criticized the self-centeredness of popular religion and its failure to recognize the reality of sin.

4.4 SEEDS OF REBELLION

4.4.1 Intellectuals

Intellectuals became increasingly critical of American life. John Kenneth Galbraith in *The Affluent Society* (1958) argued that the public sector was underfunded. John Keats's *The Crack in the Picture Window* (1956) criticized the homogeneity of suburban life in the new mass-produced communities. The adequacy of American education was questioned by James B. Conant in *The American High School Today* (1959).

4.4.2 Theatre and Fiction

Arthur Miller's *Death of a Salesman* (1949) explored the theme of the loneliness of the other-directed person. Novels also took up the conflict between the individual and mass society. Notable works included J.D. Salinger's *The Catcher in the Rye* (1951), James Jones's, *From Here to Eternity* (1951), Joseph Heller's *Catch-22* (1955), Saul Bellow's *The Adventures of Augie March* (1953), and John Updike's *Rabbit, Run* (1960).

4.4.3 Art

Painter Edward Hopper portrayed isolated, anonymous individuals. Jackson Pollock, Robert Motherwell, Willem deKooning, Arshile Gorky, and Mark Rothko were among the leaders in abstract expressionism, in which they attempted spontaneous expression of their subjectivity.

4.4.4 The Beats

The Beats were a group of young men alienated by twentieth century life. Their movement began in Greenwich Village in New York City with the friendship of Allen Ginsburg, Jack Kerouac, William Burroughs, and Neal Cassady. They emphasized alcohol, drugs, sex, jazz, Buddhism, and a restless vagabond life, all of which were vehicles for their subjectivity. Ginsberg's long poem *Howl* (1956) and Kerouac's novel *On the Road* (1957) were among their more important literary works.

CHAPTER 5

THE LIBERAL REVIVAL, 1960 – 1969

5.1 KENNEDY'S "NEW FRONTIER"

5.1.1 Legislative Failures

Kennedy was unable to get much of his program through Congress because of the alliance of Republicans and Southern Democrats. He proposed plans for federal aid to education, urban renewal, medical care for the aged, reductions in personal and corporate income taxes, and the creation of a Department of Urban Affairs. None of these proposals passed.

5.1.2 Minimum Wage

Kennedy gained congressional approval for raising the minimum wage from $1.00 to $1.25 an hour and extending it to 3 million more workers.

5.1.3 Area Redevelopment Act

The Area Redevelopment Act of 1961 made available nearly $400 million in loans to "distressed areas."

5.1.4 *Housing Act*

The 1961 Housing Act provided nearly $5 billion over four years for the preservation of open urban spaces, development of mass transit, and the construction of middle class housing.

5.1.5 *Steel Prices*

In 1961 Kennedy "jawboned" the steel industry into overturning a price increase after having encouraged labor to lower its wage demands.

5.2 CIVIL RIGHTS

5.2.1 *Freedom Riders*

In May 1961, blacks and whites, sponsored by the Congress on Racial Equality, boarded buses in Washington, D.C., traveling across the South to New Orleans to test federal enforcement of regulations prohibiting discrimination. They met violence in Alabama but continued to New Orleans. Others came into the South to test the segregation laws.

5.2.2 *Justice Department*

The Justice Department, under Attorney General Robert F. Kennedy, began to push civil rights, including desegregation of interstate transportation in the South, integration of schools, and oversight of elections.

5.2.3 *Mississippi*

In the fall of 1962 President Kennedy called the Mississippi National Guard to federal duty to enable a black, James Meredith, to enroll at the University of Mississippi.

5.2.4 *March on Washington*

Kennedy presented a comprehensive civil rights bill to Congress in 1963. It banned racial discrimination in public accommodations, gave the attorney general power to bring suits in behalf of individuals for school integration, and withheld federal funds from state-administered programs that practiced discrimination. With the bill held up in Congress, 200,000 people marched, demonstrating in its behalf on August 28, 1963, in Washington, D.C., Martin Luther King gave his "I Have a Dream" speech.

5.3 THE COLD WAR CONTINUES

5.3.1 *Bay of Pigs*

Under Eisenhower, the Central Intelligence Agency had begun training some 2,000 men for an invasion of Cuba to overthrow Fidel Castro, the left-leaning revolutionary who had taken power in 1959. On April 19, 1961, this force invaded at the Bay of Pigs but was pinned down and forced to surrender. Some 1,200 men were captured.

5.3.2 *Berlin Wall*

After a confrontation between Kennedy and Khrushchev in Berlin, Kennedy called up reserve and National Guard units and asked for an increase in defense funds. In August 1961 Khrushchev in response closed the border between East and West Berlin and ordered the erection of the Berlin Wall.

5.3.3 *Nuclear Testing*

The Soviet Union began testing of nuclear weapons in September 1961. Kennedy then authorized resumption of underground testing by the U.S.

5.3.4 Cuban Missile Crisis

On October 14, 1962, a U-2 reconnaissance plane brought photographic evidence that missile sites were being built in Cuba. Kennedy, on October 22, announced a blockade of Cuba and called on Khrushchev to dismantle the missile bases and remove all weapons capable of attacking the U.S. from Cuba. Six days later Khrushchev backed down, withdrew the missiles, and Kennedy lifted the blockade.

5.3.5 Hot Line

A "hot line" telephone connection was soon established between the White House and the Kremlin.

5.3.6 Nuclear Test Ban

In July 1963, a treaty banning the atmospheric testing of nuclear weapons was signed by all the major powers except France and China.

5.3.7 Alliance for Progress

In 1961 Kennedy announced the Alliance for Progress, which would provide $20 million in aid to Latin America.

5.3.8 Peace Corps

The Peace Corps, established in 1961, sent young volunteers to third world countries to contribute their skills in locally sponsored projects.

5.4 JOHNSON AND THE GREAT SOCIETY

5.4.1 Kennedy Assassination

On November 22, 1963, Kennedy was assassinated by Lee Harvey Oswald in Dallas, Texas. Jack Ruby, a nightclub owner, killed Oswald two days later. Conspiracy theories emerged. Chief Justice Earl Warren led an investigation of the murder and concluded that Oswald had acted alone, but questions continued.

5.4.2 Lyndon Johnson

Succeeding Kennedy, Johnson had extensive experience in both the House and Senate and, as a Texan, was the first Southerner to serve as president since Woodrow Wilson. He pushed hard for Kennedy's programs, which were languishing in Congress.

5.4.3 Tax Cut

A tax cut of over $10 billion passed Congress in 1964 and an economic boom resulted.

5.4.4 Civil Rights Act

The 1964 Civil Rights Act outlawed racial discrimination by employers and unions, created the Equal Employment Opportunity Commission to enforce the law, and eliminated the remaining restrictions on black voting.

5.4.5 Economic Opportunity Act

Michael Harrington's *The Other America* (1962) showed that 20 to 25% of American families were living below the governmentally defined poverty line. This poverty was created by increased numbers of old and young, job displacement produced by advancing technology, and regions bypassed by economic development. The Economic Opportunity Act of 1964 sought to address these problems by establishing a Job Corps, community action programs, educational programs, work-study programs, job training, loans for small businesses and farmers, and Volunteers in Service to America (VISTA), a "domestic peace corps." The Office of Economic Opportunity administered many of these programs.

5.4.6 Election of 1964

Lyndon Johnson was nominated for president by the Democrats with Senator Hubert H. Humphrey of Minnesota for vice president. The Republicans nominated Senator Barry Goldwater, a conservative from Arizona. Johnson won over 61% of the popular vote and could now launch his own "Great Society" program.

5.4.7 Health Care

The Medicare Act of 1965 combined hospital insurance for retired people with a voluntary plan to cover physician's bills. Medicaid provided grants to states to help the poor below retirement age.

5.4.8 Education

In 1965 the Elementary and Secondary Education Act provided $1.5 billion to school districts to improve the education of poor people. Head Start prepared educationally disadvantaged children for elementary school.

5.4.9 Immigration

The Immigration Act of 1965 discontinued the national origin system, basing immigration instead on such things as skills and need for political asylum.

5.4.10 Cities

The 1965 Housing and Urban Development Act provided 240,000 housing units and $2.9 billion for urban renewal. The Department of Housing and Urban Affairs was established in 1966, and rent supplements for low income families also became available.

5.4.11 Appalachia

The Appalachian Regional Development Act of 1966 provided $1.1 billion for isolated mountain areas.

5.4.12 *Space*

Fulfilling a goal established by Kennedy, Neil Armstrong and Edwin Aldrin on July 20, 1969, became the first humans to walk on the moon.

5.5 EMERGENCE OF BLACK POWER

5.5.1 *Voting Rights*

In 1965, Martin Luther King announced a voter registration drive. With help from the federal courts, he dramatized his effort by leading a march from Selma to Montgomery, Alabama, between March 21 and 25. The Voting Rights Act of 1965 authorized the U.S. attorney general to appoint officials to register voters.

5.5.2 *Racial Riots*

70% of American blacks lived in central city ghettoes. It did not appear that the tactics used in the South would help them. Frustration built up. In August 1965, the Watts section of Los Angeles erupted in a riot. More than 15,000 members of the National Guard were brought in; 34 people were killed, 850 wounded, and 3,100 arrested. Property damage totaled $200 million. In 1966, New York and Chicago experienced riots; the next year saw rioting break out in Newark and Detroit. The Kerner Commission, appointed to investigate this unrest, concluded that the riots were directed at a social system that kept blacks from getting good jobs and crowded them into ghettoes.

5.5.3 *Black Power*

By 1964 SNCC Chairman Stokely Carmichael was unwilling to work with white civil rights activists. In 1966 he called for the civil rights movements to be "black-staffed, black-controlled, and black-financed." Later he moved on to the Black Panthers, self-styled urban revolutionaries based in Oakland, California. Other leaders such as H. Rap Brown also called for Black Power.

5.5.4 King Assassination

On April 4, 1968, the Rev. Martin Luther King, Jr. was assassinated in Memphis. James Earl Ray pleaded guilty to the murder, but would later retract his plea and try to appeal his conviction, a drama that continued to unfold almost three decades later, in 1997. Riots broke out in over 100 cities following the assassination.

5.5.5 Black Officials

Despite the rising tide of violence, the number of blacks achieving elected and appointed office increased. Among the more prominent were Associate Justice of the Supreme Court Thurgood Marshall, Secretary of Housing and Urban Affairs Robert Weaver, and Senator Edward W. Brooke.

5.6 ETHNIC ACTIVISM

5.6.1 Hispanics

The number of Hispanics grew from 3 million in 1960 to 9 million in 1970 to 20 million in 1980. They were made up of Mexican-Americans (Chicanos) in California and the Southwest, Puerto Ricans in the Northeast, and Cubans in Florida.

5.6.2 United Farm Workers

Cesar Chavez founded the United Farm Workers' Organizing Committee to unionize Mexican-American farm laborers. He turned a grape pickers strike in Delano, California into a national campaign for attacking the structure of the migrant labor system through a boycott of grapes. The UFW gained recognition from the grape growers in 1970.

5.6.3 Native Americans

The American Indian Movement (AIM) was founded in 1968. Initially staging sit-ins to dramatize Indian demands, by the early 1970's it was turning to the courts for redress.

5.7 THE NEW LEFT

5.7.1 Demographic Origins

By the mid-1960's the majority of Americans were under age 30. College enrollments increased fourfold between 1945 and 1970. Universities became multiversities, often perceived as bureaucracies indifferent to student needs.

5.7.2 Students for a Democratic Society

Students for a Democratic Society was organized by Tom Hayden and Al Haber of the University of Michigan in 1960. Hayden's Port Huron Statement (1962) called for "participatory democracy." SDS drew much of its ideology from the writings of C. Wright Mills, Paul Goodman, and Herbert Marcuse.

5.7.3 Free Speech Movement

In 1964 students at the University of California at Berkeley staged free speech sit-ins to protest the prohibition of political canvassing on campus. Led by Mario Savio, the free speech movement shifted from emphasizing student rights to criticizing the bureaucracy of American society. In December police broke up a sit-in, and protests were sparked on other campuses across the U.S.

5.7.4 Vietnam

Student protests began focusing on the Vietnam War. In the spring of 1967, 500,000 gathered in Central Park in New York

City to protest the war, many burning their draft cards. SDS became more militant, willing to use violence and turning to Lenin for its ideology.

5.7.5 *1968*

More than 200 large campus demonstrations took place in the spring, culminating in the occupation of buildings at Columbia University in New York to protest the university's poor relations with minority groups and its involvement in military research. Police wielding clubs eventually broke up the demonstration. In August thousands gathered in Chicago to protest the war during the Democratic Convention. Although police violence against the demonstrators aroused anger, the anti-war movement began to split into pro- and anti-violence camps.

5.7.6 *Decline*

Beginning in 1968, SDS began breaking up into rival factions. After the more radical factions began using bombs, Tom Hayden left the group. By the early 1970's the New Left had lost political influence, having abandoned its original commitment to democracy and non-violence.

5.8 THE COUNTERCULTURE

5.8.1 *Origins*

Like the New Left, the founders of the counterculture were alienated by bureaucracy, materialism, and the Vietnam War, but they turned away from politics in favor of an alternative society. In many respects, they were heirs of the Beats, who had expressed broad disillusionment with the Cold War.

5.8.2 *Counterculture Expression*

Many young people formed communes in such places as San Francisco's Haight-Ashbury district or in rural areas. "Hippies," as they were called, experimented with Eastern religions, drugs, and sex, but most were unable to establish a self-sustaining lifestyle. Leading spokesmen included Timothy Leary, Theodore Roszak, and Charles Reich.

5.8.3 Woodstock

Rock music was a major element of the counterculture. The Woodstock Music Festival, held in August 1969 in upstate New York featured such musicians as Joan Baez, Jimi Hendrix, and Santana and offered opportunity for unrestrained drug use and sex. In contrast to the joy of Woodstock was the slaying, in full view of the audience, of a concertgoer a few months later at the Altamont Speedway in California. By the early 1970's the counterculture was shrinking, either as the victim of its own excesses or by way of absorption into the mainstream.

5.9 WOMEN'S LIBERATION

5.9.1 Betty Friedan

In *The Feminine Mystique* (1963) Betty Friedan argued that middle-class society stifled women and did not allow them to use their individual talents. She attacked what she described as the cult of domesticity.

5.9.2 National Organization for Women

Friedan and other feminists founded the National Organization for Women (NOW) in 1966, calling for equal employment opportunities and equal pay.

5.9.3 Expanding Demands

In 1967 NOW advocated an Equal Rights Amendment to the Constitution, changes in divorce laws, and legalization of abortion. In 1972 the federal government required colleges receiving federal funds to establish "affirmative action" programs for women to ensure equal opportunity, and the following year the Supreme Court legalized abortion in *Roe v. Wade.*

5.9.4 *Problems*

The women's movement was largely limited to the middle class. The Equal Rights Amendment failed to pass. And abortion rights stirred up a counter "right-to-life" movement.

5.10 THE SEXUAL REVOLUTION

5.10.1 *Sexual Practices*

In 1948 Alfred C. Kinsey published pioneering research indicating widespread variation in sexual practices. In the 1960's new methods of birth control, particularly the "pill," and antibiotics encouraged freer sexual practices and challenges to traditional taboos against premarital sex.

5.10.2 *Homosexual Rights*

Gay and lesbian rights activists emerged in the 1960's and 1970's, particularly after a 1969 police raid on the Stonewall Inn, a homosexual hangout in New York City's Greenwich Village.

5.11 CULTURAL EXPRESSIONS

5.11.1 *Movies*

American films achieved a higher level of maturity. *Who's Afraid of Virginia Woolf* (1966) and *The Graduate* (1967) questioned dominant social values. *Dr. Strangelove* (1964) satirized the military establishment while *Bonnie and Clyde* (1969) glamorized two bank robbers. *Easy Rider* (1969) portrayed the counterculture. The dehumanizing aspects of technology were dramatized in *2001: A Space Odyssey* (1968).

5.11.2 *Literature*

Truman Capote's *In Cold Blood* (1965), Norman Mailer's

Armies of the Night (1968), and Tom Wolfe's *Electric Kool-Aid Acid Test* (1968) combined factual and fictional elements.

5.11.3 *Art*

Pop artists such as Andy Warhol, Roy Lichtenstein, and Claes Oldenburg drew their subjects out of such elements of popular culture as advertising, comics, and hamburgers.

5.11.4 *Theatre*

Much theatre became experimental as exemplified by the San Francisco Mime Troupe. Some plays, including Barbara Garson's *MacBird* (1966) and Arthur Kopit's *Indians* (1969) took an explicitly radical political stance.

5.12 VIETNAM

5.12.1 *Background*

After the French defeat in 1954, the United States sent military advisors to South Vietnam to aid the government of Ngo Dinh Diem. The pro-communist Vietcong forces gradually grew in strength, partly because Diem failed to follow through on promised reforms. They received support from North Vietnam, the Soviet Union, and China. The U.S. government supported a successful military coup against Diem in the fall of 1963. The number of U.S. military advisors increased from 2,000 in 1961 to 16,000 at the time of John F. Kennedy's death.

5.12.2 *Escalation*

In August 1964 – after claiming that North Vietnamese gunboats had fired on American destroyers in the Gulf of Tonkin – Lyndon Johnson pushed the Gulf of Tonkin resolution through Congress which authorized him to use military force in Vietnam. After a February 1965 attack by the Vietcong on Pleiku, Johnson ordered operation "Rolling Thunder," the first sustained bombing of North Vietnam. Johnson then sent combat troops to South Vietnam; under the leadership of Gen-

THE VIETNAM WAR, 1964 – 1975

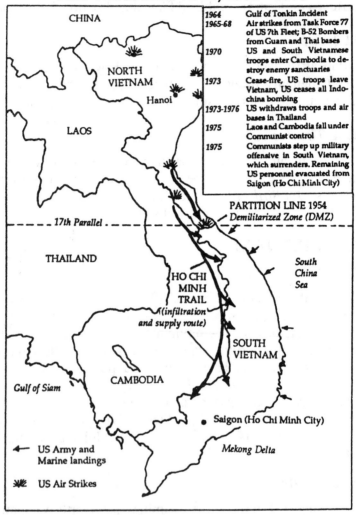

1964	Gulf of Tonkin Incident
1965-68	Air strikes from Task Force 77 of US 7th Fleet; B-52 Bombers from Guam and Thai bases
1970	US and South Vietnamese troops enter Cambodia to destroy enemy sanctuaries
1973	Cease-fire, US troops leave Vietnam, US ceases all Indochina bombing
1973-1976	US withdraws troops and air bases in Thailand
1975	Laos and Cambodia fall under Communist control
1975	Communists step up military offensive in South Vietnam, which surrenders. Remaining US personnel evacuated from Saigon (Ho Chi Minh City)

CHINA

NORTH VIETNAM

Hanoi

LAOS

PARTITION LINE 1954
Demilitarized Zone (DMZ)

— — — 17th Parallel — — —

THAILAND

HO CHI MINH TRAIL
(infiltration and supply route)

South China Sea

SOUTH VIETNAM

Gulf of Siam

CAMBODIA

• Saigon (Ho Chi Minh City)

◄— US Army and Marine landings

Mekong Delta

※ US Air Strikes

eral William C. Westmoreland, they conducted search and destroy operations. The number of troops increased to 184,000 in 1965; 385,000 in 1966; 485,000 in 1967, and 538,000 in 1968. Increases in the number of American troops were met by increases in the number of North Vietnamese fighting with the Vietcong and increased aid from the Soviet Union and China.

5.12.3 Defense of American Policy

"Hawks" defended the president's policy and, drawing on containment theory, said that the nation had the responsibility to resist aggression. Secretary of State Dean Rusk became a major spokesman for the domino theory, which justified government policy by analogy with England's and France's failure to stop Hitler prior to 1939. If Vietnam should fall, it was said, all Southeast Asia would eventually go. The administration stressed the U.S. willingness to negotiate the withdrawal of all "foreign" forces from the war.

5.12.4 Opposition

Opposition began quickly, with "teach-ins" at the University of Michigan in 1965, and a 1966 congressional investigation led by Senator J. William Fulbright. Antiwar demonstrations were gaining large crowds by 1967. "Doves" argued that the war was a civil war in which the U.S. should not meddle. They said that the South Vietnamese regimes were not democratic, and opposed large-scale aerial bombings, use of chemical weapons, and the killing of civilians. Doves rejected the domino theory, pointing to the growing losses of American life (over 40,000 by 1970) and the economic cost of the war.

5.12.5 Tet Offensive

On January 31, 1968, the first day of the Vietnamese new year (Tet), the Vietcong attacked numerous cities and towns, American bases, and even Saigon. Although they suffered large losses, the Vietcong won a psychological victory as American opinion began turning against the war.

5.13 ELECTION OF 1968

5.13.1 Eugene McCarthy

In November 1967 Senator Eugene McCarthy of Minnesota announced his candidacy for the 1968 Democratic presidential nomination, running on the issue of opposition to the war.

5.13.2 New Hampshire

In February, McCarthy won 42% of the Democratic vote in the New Hampshire primary, compared with Johnson's 48%. Robert F. Kennedy then announced his candidacy for the Democratic presidential nomination.

5.13.3 Johnson's Withdrawal

Lyndon Johnson withdrew his candidacy on March 31, 1968, and Vice President Hubert H. Humphrey took his place as a candidate for the Democratic nomination.

5.13.4 Kennedy Assassination

After winning the California primary over McCarthy, Robert Kennedy was assassinated by Sirhan Sirhan, a young Palestinian. This event assured Humphrey's nomination.

5.13.5 The Nominees

The Republicans nominated Richard M. Nixon, who chose Spiro T. Agnew, Governor of Maryland, as his running mate in order to appeal to Southern voters. Governor George C. Wallace of Alabama ran for the presidency under the banner of the American Independent party, appealing to fears generated by protestors and big government. The Democrats nominated Humphrey at their convention in Chicago, while outside the convention hall police and anti-war activists clashed.

5.13.6 Nixon's Victory

Johnson suspended air attacks on North Vietnam shortly before the election. Nonetheless, Nixon, who emphasized stability and order, defeated Humphrey by a margin of 1%. Wallace's 13.5% was the best showing by a third-party candidate since 1924.

CHAPTER 6

THE NIXON REACTION, 1969 – 1974

6.1 NIXON CONSERVATISM

6.1.1 *Civil Rights*

The Nixon Administration sought to block renewal of the Voting Rights Act and delay implementation of court-ordered school desegregation in Mississippi. After the Supreme Court ordered busing of students in 1971 to achieve school desegregation, the administration proposed an anti-busing bill which was blocked in Congress.

6.1.2 *Supreme Court*

In 1969 Nixon appointed Warren E. Burger, a conservative, as Chief Justice but ran into opposition with the nomination of Southerners Clement F. Haynesworth, Jr. and G. Harrold Carswell. After these nominations were defeated, he nominated Harry A. Blackmun, who received Senate approval. He later appointed Lewis F. Powell, Jr. and William Rehnquist as associate justices. Although more conservative than the Warren court, the Burger court did declare the death penalty, as used at the time, as unconstitutional in 1972 and struck down state anti-abortion legislation in 1973.

6.1.3 Revenue Sharing

The heart of Nixon's "New Federalism," Congress passed in 1972 a five year plan to distribute $30 billion of federal revenues to the states.

6.1.4 Welfare

Nixon proposed that the bulk of welfare payments be shifted to the states and that a "minimum income" be established for poor families, but did not push the program through Congress.

6.1.5 Congressional Legislation

Congress passed bills giving 18-year-olds the right to vote (1970), increasing Social Security benefits and funding for food stamps (1970), the Occupational Safety and Health Act (1970), the Clean Air Act (1970), acts to control water pollution (1970, 1972), and the Federal Election Campaign Act (1972). None were supported by the Nixon administration.

6.1.6 Economic Problems

Unemployment climbed to 6% in 1970, real gross national product declined in 1970, and in 1971 the U.S. experienced a trade deficit. Inflation reached 12% by 1974. These problems resulted from federal deficits in the 1960's, international competition, and rising energy costs.

6.1.7 Economic Policy

In 1969, Nixon cut spending and raised taxes. He then encouraged the Federal Reserve Board to raise interest rates. The economy worsened. In 1970 Congress gave the president the power to regulate prices and wages. Nixon used this power in August 1971 to impose a 90-day price and wage freeze and to take the U.S. off the gold standard. At the end of the ninety days he established mandatory guidelines for wage and price increases. Finally, in 1973 he turned to voluntary wage and price controls except on health care, food, and construction. When inflation increased rapidly, Nixon cut back on government expenditures, refusing to spend (impound) funds already appropriated by Congress.

6.2 VIETNAMIZATION

6.2.1 First Proposal

Nixon first proposed that all non-South Vietnamese troops be withdrawn in phases and that an internationally supervised election be held in South Vietnam. The North Vietnamese rejected this plan.

6.2.2 Vietnamization

The president then turned to "Vietnamization," the effort to build up South Vietnamese forces while withdrawing American troops. In 1969 Nixon reduced American troop strength by 60,000, but at the same time ordered the bombing of Cambodia, a neutral country.

6.2.3 Protests

Two Moratorium Days in 1969 brought out several hundred thousand protestors, and reports of an American massacre of Vietnamese at My Lai reignited controversy over the nature of the war, but Nixon continued to defend his policy. Troop withdrawals continued, and a lottery system was instituted in 1970 to make the draft more equitable. In 1973 Nixon abolished the draft and established an all-volunteer army.

6.2.4 Cambodia

In April 1970, Nixon announced that Vietnamization was succeeding and that another 150,000 American troops would be out of Vietnam by the end of the year. A few days later, he sent troops into Cambodia to clear out Vietcong sanctuaries and resumed bombing of North Vietnam.

6.2.5 Kent State

Protests against escalation of the war were especially strong on college campuses. During a May 1970 demonstration at Kent State University in Ohio, the National Guard opened fire on protestors, killing four students. Soon after, two black students were killed by a Mississippi state policeman at Jackson State University. Several hundred colleges were soon closed down by student strikes as moderates joined the radicals. Congress repealed the Gulf of Tonkin Resolution.

6.2.6 Pentagon Papers

The publication in the press in 1971 of "The Pentagon Papers," classified Defense Department documents, revealed that the government had misled the Congress and the American people regarding its intentions in Vietnam during the mid-1960's.

6.2.7 Mining

Nixon drew American forces back from Cambodia but increased bombing. In March 1972, after stepped-up aggression from the North, Nixon ordered the mining of Haiphong and other northern ports.

6.2.8 End of U.S. Involvement

In the summer of 1972 negotiations between the U.S. and North Vietnam began in Paris. A draft agreement was developed by October which included a cease-fire, return of American prisoners of war, and withdrawal of U.S. forces from Vietnam. A few days before the 1972 presidential election, Henry Kissinger, the president's national security advisor, announced that peace was at hand.

6.2.9   Resumed Bombing

Nixon resumed bombing of North Vietnam in December 1972, claiming that the North Vietnamese were not bargaining in good faith. In January 1973 the opponents reached a settlement in which the North Vietnamese retained control over large areas of the South and agreed to release American prisoners of war within 60 days. After the prisoners were released, the U.S. would withdraw its remaining troops. Nearly 60,000 Americans had been killed and 300,000 more were wounded, while the war had cost Americans $109 billion. On March 29, 1973, the last American combat troops left South Vietnam.

6.3   FOREIGN POLICY

6.3.1   China

Along with his national security advisor, Nixon took some bold diplomatic initiatives. Kissinger traveled to China and the Soviet Union for secret sessions to plan summit meetings with the communists. In February 1972, Nixon and Kissinger went to China to meet with Mao Tse-tung and his associates. The U.S. agreed to support China's admission to the United Nations and to pursue economic and cultural exchanges. These decisions ended the refusal of the U.S. to accept the Chinese revolution.

6.3.2   Soviet Union

At a May 1972 meeting with Soviet leaders, a Strategic Arms Limitation Treaty (SALT) was signed. In this treaty, the signatories agreed to stop making nuclear ballistic missiles and to reduce the number of antiballistic missiles to 200 for each power.

6.3.3 *Détente*

Nixon and Kissinger called their policy *détente*, a French term which meant a relaxation in the tensions between two governments. The policy sought to establish rules to govern the rivalry between the U.S. and China and the Soviet Union. The agreements were significant in part because they were made before the U.S. withdrew from Vietnam.

6.3.4 *Middle East*

Following the Arab-Israeli war of 1973, the Arab states established an oil boycott to push the western nations into forcing Israel to withdraw from lands controlled since the "six day" war of 1967. Kissinger, now secretary of state, negotiated the withdrawal of Israel from some of the lands and the Arabs lifted their boycott. The Organization of Petroleum Exporting Countries (OPEC) – Venezuela, Saudi Arabia, Kuwait, Iraq, and Iran – then raised the price of oil from about $3.00 to $11.65 a barrel. U.S. gas prices doubled and inflation shot above 10%.

6.4 ELECTION OF 1972

6.4.1 *George McGovern*

The Democrats nominated Senator George McGovern of South Dakota for president and Senator Thomas Eagleton for vice president. After the press revealed that Eagleton had previously been treated for psychological problems, McGovern eventually forced him off the ticket, replacing him with Sargent Shriver. McGovern was also hampered by a party divided over the war and social policies as well as his own relative radicalism.

6.4.2 George Wallace

Wallace ran again as the American Independent Party candidate but was shot on May 15 and left paralyzed below the waist.

6.4.3 Richard M. Nixon

Richard M. Nixon and Spiro T. Agnew, who had been renominated by the Republicans, won a landslide victory, with an electoral vote margin of 521 to 17. This mandate held the potential for Nixon to become one of the most powerful presidents in U.S. history.

6.5 WATERGATE

6.5.1 The Break-In

What became known as the Watergate crisis began during the 1972 presidential campaign. Early on the morning of June 17, James McCord, a security officer for the Committee to Reelect the President (CRP), and four other men broke into Democratic headquarters at the Watergate apartment complex in Washington, D.C., and were caught while going through files and installing electronic eavesdropping devices. On June 22, Nixon announced that the administration was in no way involved in the burglary attempt.

6.5.2 James McCord

The trial of the burglars began in early 1973, with all but McCord, who was convicted, pleading guilty. Before sentencing, McCord wrote a letter to U.S. District Court Judge John J. Sirica arguing that high Republican officials had known in advance about the burglary and that perjury had been committed at the trial.

6.5.3 Further Revelations

Soon Jeb Stuart Magruder, head of CRP, and John W.

Dean, Nixon's attorney, stated that they had been involved. Dean testified before a Senate Watergate investigating committee that Nixon had been involved in covering up the incident. Over the next several months, extensive involvement of the administration, including payment of "silence" money to the burglars, destruction of FBI records, forgery of documents, and wiretapping, was revealed. Dean was fired and H.R. Haldeman and John Ehrlichman, who headed the White House Staff, and Attorney General Richard Kleindienst, resigned. Nixon claimed that he had not personally been involved in the cover-up but refused, on the grounds of executive privilege, to allow investigation of White House documents.

6.5.4 *White House Tapes*

Under considerable pressure, Nixon agreed to the appointment of a special prosecutor, Archibald Cox of Harvard Law School. When Cox obtained a subpoena for tape recordings of White House conversations (whose existence had been revealed during the Senate hearings) – and the administration lost an appeal in the appellate court – Nixon ordered Elliot Richardson, now the attorney general, to fire Cox. Both Richardson and his subordinate, William Ruckelshaus, resigned, leaving Robert Bork, the solicitor general, to carry out the order. This "Saturday Night Massacre," which took place on October 20, 1973, aroused a storm of controversy. The House Judiciary Committee, headed by Peter Rodino of New Jersey, began looking into the possibilities of impeachment. Nixon agreed to turn the tapes over to Judge Sirica and named Leon Jaworski as the new special prosecutor. But it soon became known that some of the tapes were missing and that a portion of another had been erased.

6.5.5 *The Vice Presidency*

Vice President Spiro Agnew was accused of income tax fraud and having accepted bribes while a local official in Maryland. He resigned the vice presidency in October 1973, and was replaced by Congressman Gerald R. Ford of Michigan under provisions of the new 25th Amendment.

6.5.6 Nixon's Taxes

Nixon was accused of paying almost no income taxes between 1969 and 1972, and of using public funds for improvements to his private residences in California and Florida. The IRS reviewed the president's tax return and assessed him nearly $500,000 in back taxes and interest.

6.5.7 Indictments

In March 1974, a grand jury indicted Haldeman, Ehrlichman, former Attorney General John Mitchell, and four other White House aides and named Nixon an unindicted co-conspirator.

6.5.8 Calls for Resignation

In April, Nixon released edited transcripts of the White House tapes, the contents of which led to further calls for his resignation. Jaworski subpoenaed 64 additional tapes, which Nixon refused to turn over, and the case went to the Supreme Court.

6.5.9 Impeachment Debate

Meanwhile, the House Judiciary Committee televised its debate over impeachment, adopting three articles of impeachment. It charged the president with obstructing justice, misusing presidential power, and failing to obey the committee's subpoenas.

6.5.10 *Resignation*

Before the House began to debate impeachment, the Supreme Court ordered the president to release the subpoenaed tapes to the special prosecutor. On August 5, Nixon, under pressure from his advisors, released the tape of June 23, 1972, to the public. This tape, recorded less than a week after the break-in, revealed that Nixon had used the CIA to keep the FBI from investigating the case. Nixon announced his resignation on August 8, 1974, to take effect at noon the following day. Gerald Ford then became president.

6.5.11 *Legislative Response*

Congress responded to the Vietnam War and Watergate by enacting legislation intended to prevent such situations. The War Powers Act (1973) required congressional approval of any commitment of combat troops beyond 90 days. In 1974 Congress limited the amounts of contributions and expenditures in presidential campaigns. And it strengthened the 1966 Freedom of Information Act by requiring the government to act promptly when asked for information and to prove its case for classification when attempting to withhold information on grounds of national security.

CHAPTER 7

YEARS OF DRIFT, 1974 – 1980

7.1 THE FORD PRESIDENCY

7.1.1 *Gerald Ford*

Gerald Ford was in many respects the opposite of Nixon. Although a partisan Republican, he was well-liked and free from any hint of scandal.

7.1.2 *Nixon Pardon*

Ford almost immediately encountered controversy when in September 1974 he pardoned Nixon, who accepted the offer, although he admitted no wrongdoing and had not yet been charged with a crime.

7.1.3 *The Economy*

Ford also faced major economic problems which he approached somewhat inconsistently. Saying that inflation was the major problem, he called for voluntary restraints and asked citizens to wear WIN (Whip Inflation Now) buttons. The economy went into decline, unemployment reaching above 9% in 1975 and the federal deficit topping $60 billion the following year. Ford asked for tax cuts to stimulate business and argued against spending for social programs.

7.1.4 . New York

When New York City approached bankruptcy in 1975, Ford at first opposed federal aid, but he changed his mind when the Senate and House Banking Committees guaranteed the loans.

7.1.5 Vietnam

As North Vietnamese forces pushed back the South Vietnamese, Ford asked Congress to provide more arms for the South. Congress rejected the request and in April 1975 Saigon fell to the North Vietnamese.

7.1.6 Seizure of the Mayaguez

On May 12, 1975, Cambodia, which had been taken over by communists two weeks earlier, seized the American merchant ship *Mayaguez* in the Gulf of Siam. After demanding that the ship and crew be freed, Ford ordered a Marine assault on Tang Island, where the ship had been taken. The ship and crew of 39 were released but 38 Marines were killed.

7.1.7 Election of 1976

Ronald Reagan, formerly a movie actor and governor of California, opposed Ford for the Republican nomination, but Ford won by a slim margin. The Democrats nominated James Earl Carter, formerly governor of Georgia, who ran on the basis of his integrity and lack of Washington connections. Carter, with Walter Mondale, senator from Minnesota, as the vice presidential candidate, defeated Ford narrowly.

7.2   CARTER'S MODERATE LIBERALISM

7.2.1   *Jimmy Carter*

Carter, who wished to be called "Jimmy," sought to conduct the presidency on democratic and moral principles. However, his administration gained a reputation for proposing complex programs to Congress and then not continuing to support them through the legislative process.

7.2.2   *The Economy*

Carter approached economic problems inconsistently. Although during the campaign he had argued that inflation needed to be restrained, in 1977 he proposed a $50 per person income tax rebate, but the idea ran into congressional resistance. In 1978 Carter proposed voluntary wage and price guidelines. Although somewhat successful, the guidelines did not apply to oil, housing, and food. Carter then named Paul A. Volcker as chairman of the Federal Reserve Board. Volcker tightened the money supply in order to reduce inflation, but this action caused interest rates to go even higher. High interest rates depressed sales of automobiles and houses which in turn increased unemployment. By 1980 unemployment stood at 7.5%, interest at 20%, and inflation at 12%.

7.2.3   *Energy*

Carter also approached energy problems inconsistently. Attempting to reduce America's growing dependence on foreign oil, in 1977 he proposed raising the tax on gasoline and taxing automobiles that used fuel inefficiently, among other things, but obtained only a gutted version of his bill. Near the end of his term, Carter proposed coupling deregulation of the price of American crude oil with a windfall profits tax, a program that pleased neither liberals nor conservatives. Energy problems were further exacerbated by a second fuel shortage which occurred in 1979.

7.2.4 Domestic Achievements

Carter offered amnesty to Americans who had fled the draft and gone to other countries during the Vietnam war. He established the Departments of Energy and Education and placed the civil service on a merit basis. He created a "superfund" for cleanup of chemical waste dumps, established controls over strip mining, and protected 100 million acres of Alaskan wilderness from development.

7.3 CARTER'S FOREIGN POLICY

7.3.1 Human Rights

Carter sought to base foreign policy on human rights but was criticized for inconsistency and lack of attention to American interests.

7.3.2 Panama Canal

Carter negotiated a controversial treaty with Panama, affirmed by the Senate in 1978, that provided for the transfer of ownership of the Canal to Panama in 1999, and guaranteed its neutrality.

7.3.3 China

Carter ended official recognition of Taiwan and in 1979 recognized the People's Republic of China. Conservatives called the decision a "sell-out."

7.3.4 SALT II

In 1979 the administration signed the Strategic Arms Limitation Treaty (SALT II) with the Soviet Union. The treaty set a ceiling of 2,250 bombers and missiles for each side and established limits on warheads and new weapons systems. It never passed the Senate.

7.3.5 *Camp David Accords*

In 1978 Carter negotiated the Camp David Accords (signed in 1979) between Israel and Egypt. Bringing Anwar Sadat, the president of Egypt, and Menachem Begin, prime minister of Israel, to Camp David for two weeks in September 1978, Carter sought to end the state of war that existed between the two countries. Israel promised to return occupied land in the Sinai to Egypt in exchange for Egyptian recognition, a process completed in 1982. An agreement to negotiate the Palestinian refugee problem proved ineffective.

7.3.6 *Afghanistan*

The policy of détente went into decline. Carter criticized Soviet restrictions on political freedom and reluctance to allow dissidents and Jews to emigrate. In December 1979 the Soviet Union invaded Afghanistan. Carter stopped shipments of grain and certain advanced technology to the Soviet Union, withdrew SALT II from the Senate, and barred Americans from competing in the 1980 summer Olympics held in Moscow.

7.4 THE IRANIAN CRISIS

7.4.1 *The Iranian Revolution*

In 1978 a revolution forced the Shah of Iran to flee the country, replacing him with a religious leader, Ayatollah Ruhollah Khomeini. Because the U.S. had supported the Shah with arms and money, the revolutionaries were strongly anti-American, calling the U.S. the "Great Satan."

7.4.2 *Hostages*

After Carter allowed the exiled Shah to come to the U.S.

for medical treatment in October 1979, some 400 Iranians broke into the American Embassy in Teheran on November 4, taking the occupants captive. They demanded that the Shah be returned to Iran for trial and that his wealth be confiscated and given to Iran. Carter rejected these demands; instead, he froze Iranian assets in the U.S. and established a trade embargo against Iran. He also appealed to the United Nations and the World Court. The Iranians eventually freed the black and women hostages but retained 52 others. At first the crisis helped Carter politically as the nation rallied in support of the hostages.

7.4.3 Rescue Attempt

With the hostage crisis continuing, Carter in April 1980 ordered a Marine rescue attempt but it collapsed after several helicopters broke down and another crashed, killing 8 men. Secretary of State Cyrus Vance resigned in protest before the raid began and Carter was widely criticized for the attempted raid.

7.4.4 The Shah

The Shah, who now lived in Egypt, died in July 1980, but this had no effect on the hostage crisis.

7.5 ELECTION OF 1980

7.5.1 The Democrats

Carter, whose standing in polls had dropped to about 25% in 1979, successfully withstood a challenge from Senator Edward M. Kennedy for the Democratic presidential nomination.

7.5.2 The Republicans

The Republicans nominated Ronald Reagan of California, who had narrowly lost the 1976 nomination and was the leading spokesman for American conservatism. Reagan chose George Bush, a New Englander transplanted to Texas and former CIA director, as his vice presidential candidate. One of Reagan's opponents, Congressman John Anderson of Illinois, continued his presidential campaign on a third party ticket.

7.5.3 *The Campaign*

While Carter defended his record, Reagan called for reductions in government spending and taxes, said he would transfer more power from the federal government to the states, and advocated what were coming to be called traditional values – family, religion, hard work, and patriotism.

7.5.4 *Reagan's Victory*

Although the election was regarded by many experts as "too close to call," Reagan won by a large electoral majority and the Republicans gained control of the Senate and increased their representation in the House.

7.5.5 *American Hostages*

After extensive negotiations with Iran, in which Algeria acted as an intermediary, Carter released Iranian assets and the hostages were freed on January 20, 1981, 444 days after being taken captive and on the day of Reagan's inauguration.

7.6 SOCIETY AND CULTURE

7.6.1 *Blacks*

A two-tier black social structure was emerging, a middle class and an "underclass" living in the ghettoes. Single parent families, usually headed by females, grew disproportionately among the black underclass.

7.6.2 Hispanics

The Hispanic population grew 61% during the 1970's, many of them "undocumented" immigrants who worked in low-paying service jobs.

7.6.3 Asians

The number of Asians – Chinese, Japanese, Filipinos, Koreans, and Vietnamese – increased rapidly during the 1970's. Disciplined and hard working, many of them moved into the middle class in a single generation.

7.6.4 Women

By 1978, 50% of all women over sixteen were employed, up from 37% in 1965. Marriages dropped from 148 per thousand women in 1960 to 108 per thousand in 1980. Divorce climbed from 2.2% in 1960 to 5.2% in 1980. During the same years, births dropped from 24 per thousand to 14.8.

7.6.5 Aging Population

The median age for Americans rose from 28 in 1970 to 30 in 1980.

7.6.6 Equal Rights Amendment

Approved by Congress in 1972, the ERA aroused opposition among traditionalists, led by Phyllis Schlafly, and was never ratified by the required 38 states.

7.6.7 Abortion

After the Supreme Court in *Roe v. Wade* (1973) legalized abortion during the first three months of pregnancy, conflict arose between "pro-choice" (those who wished to keep abortion legal) and "pro-life" (those who were anti-abortion) groups. The issue affected many local and state political campaigns.

7.6.8 Population Shift

Population was shifting from the Northeast to the "Sunbelt," represented by such states as Florida, Texas, Arizona, and California. When Congress was reapportioned following the 1980 census, these four states gained representation while New York, Illinois, Ohio, and Pennsylvania lost seats. The Sunbelt tended to be politically conservative.

7.6.9 Narcissism

In contrast to the social consciousness of the 1960's, the 1970's were often described as the time of the "me generation." Writers such as Tom Wolfe and Christopher Lasch described a "culture of narcissism," in which preoccupation with the self appeared in the popularity of personal fulfillment programs, health and exercise fads, and even religious cults.

7.6.10 Religion

During the 1970's the U.S. experienced a major revival of conservative Christianity, spread among both the fundamentalists and the more moderate evangelicals. A 1977 survey suggested that some 70 million Americans considered themselves "born-again" Christians, the most prominent of whom was President Jimmy Carter, a devout Baptist. Many of these Christians, led by the Reverend Jerry Falwell's "Moral Majority," became politically active, favoring prayer and the teaching of creationism in the public schools, opposing abortion, pornography, and the ERA, and supporting a strong national defense.

7.6.11 Literature

Saul Bellow's *Mr. Sammler's Planet* (1970) reflected on the moral and spiritual dimensions of contemporary society. Thomas Pynchon pursued avant garde uses of fiction in *Gravity's Rainbow*

(1973). Robert Stone reexamined the Vietnam experience in *Dog Soldiers* (1975), while Alex Haley recounted his black family's origins in *Roots* (1976), which was later produced as a major television miniseries. E.L. Doctorow's *Ragtime* (1975) mixed fact and fiction in retelling the history of America in the early 1900's.

7.6.12 Film

Francis Ford Coppola began his history of a Mafia family with *The Godfather* (1972). George Lucas examined the end of 1950's innocence in *American Graffiti* (1973) and opened his *Star Wars* (1977) series. *One Flew Over the Cuckoo's Nest* (1975) questioned concepts of insanity and normality. Toward the end of the decade, images of the Vietnam War appeared in *The Deer Hunter* (1978), *Coming Home* (1978), and *Apocalypse Now* (1979).

7.6.13 Art

Richard Estes' "Central Savings" (1975) exemplified what critics termed the "New Realism." Audrey Rack combined traditional painting and photography in "Queen" (1976).

7.6.14 Music and Theater

Leonard Bernstein's *Mass* (1971) eclectically combined both religious traditions and musical styles. Composer Philip Glass and artist Robert Wilson combined their talents in the opera *Einstein on the Beach* (1976). Comedy writer Neil Simon introduced *Last of the Red-Hot Lovers* (1970) and Stephen Sondheim extended the tradition of the American musical with *A Little Night Music* (1973).

CHAPTER 8

THE CONSERVATIVE
REVOLUTION, 1981 – 1991

8.1 REAGAN ATTACKS
BIG GOVERNMENT

8.1.1 *Tax Policy*

An ideological though pragmatic conservative, Ronald Reagan acted quickly and forcefully to change the direction of government policy. He placed priority on cutting taxes. His approach was based on "supply-side" economics, the idea that if government left more money in the hands of the people, they would invest rather then spend the excess on consumer goods. The results would be greater production, more jobs, and greater prosperity, and thus more income for the government despite lower tax rates.

8.1.2 *Economic Recovery Tax Act*

Reagan asked for a 30% tax cut and, despite fears of inflation on the part of Congress, in August 1983 obtained a 25%

cut, spread over three years. The percentage was the same for everyone; hence high income people received greater savings than middle and low income individuals. To encourage investment, capital gains, gift, and inheritance taxes were reduced and business taxes liberalized. Anyone with earned income was also allowed to invest up to $2,000 a year in an individual retirement account (IRA), deferring all taxes on both the principle and its earnings until retirement.

8.1.3 Government Spending

Congress passed the Budget Reconciliation Act in 1981, cutting $39 billion from domestic programs, including education, food stamps, public housing, and the National Endowments for the Arts and Humanities. Reagan said that he would maintain a "safety net" for the "truly needy," focusing aid on those unable to work because of disability or need for child care. While cutting domestic programs, Reagan increased the defense budget by $12 billion.

8.1.4 Economic Response

By December 1982, the economy was experiencing recession because of the Federal Reserve's "tight money" policy, with over 10% unemployment. From a deficit of $59 billion in 1980, the federal budget was running $195 billion in the red by 1983. The rate of inflation, however, helped by lower demand for goods and services and an oversupply of oil as non-OPEC countries increased production, fell from a high of 12% in 1979 to 4% in 1984. The Federal Reserve Board then began to lower interest rates which together with lower inflation and more spendable income because of lower taxes, resulted in more business activity. Unemployment fell to less than 8%.

8.1.5 Increasing Revenue

Because of rising deficits, Reagan and Congress increased

taxes in various ways. The 1982 Tax Equity and Fiscal Responsibility Act reversed some concessions made to business in 1981. Social Security benefits became taxable income in 1983. In 1984 the Deficit Reduction Act increased taxes by another $50 billion. But the deficit continued to increase.

8.1.6 Air Traffic Controllers

The federally employed air traffic controllers entered an illegal strike in August 1981. After Reagan ordered them to return to work, and most refused to do so, the president then fired them, 11,400 in all, effectively destroying their union, and began training replacements.

8.1.7 Assassination Attempt

John W. Hinckley shot Reagan in the chest on March 30, 1981. The president was seriously wounded but handled the incident with humor and made a swift recovery. His popularity increased, possibly helping his legislative program.

8.1.8 Antitrust

Reagan ended ongoing federal antitrust suits against IBM and AT&T, thereby fulfilling his promise to reduce government interference with business.

8.1.9 Women and Minorities

Although Reagan appointed Sandra Day O'Connor to the Supreme Court, his administration gave fewer of its appointments to women and minorities than had the Carter administration. The Reagan administration also opposed "equal pay for equal work" and renewal of the Voting Rights Act of 1965.

8.1.10 *Problems with Appointed Officials*

A number of Reagan appointees were accused of conflict of interest, including Anne Gorsuch Burford and Rita Lavelle of the Environmental Protection Agency, Edwin Meese, presidential advisor and later attorney general, and Michael Deaver, the deputy chief of staff. Ray Donovan, secretary of labor, was indicted but acquitted of charges that he had made payoffs to government officials while he was in private business. By the end of Reagan's term, more than 100 of his officials had been accused of questionable activities.

8.2 REAGAN ASSERTS AMERICAN POWER

8.2.1 *Soviet Union*

Reagan took a hard line against the Soviet Union, calling it an "evil empire." He placed new cruise missiles in Europe, despite considerable opposition from Europeans.

8.2.2 *Latin America*

Reagan encouraged the opposition (*contras*) to the leftist Sandinista government of Nicaragua with arms, tactical support, and intelligence and supplied aid to the government of El Salvador in its struggles against left-wing rebels. In October 1983 the president also sent American troops into the Caribbean Island of Grenada to overthrow a newly established Cuban-backed regime.

8.2.3 *Middle East*

As the Lebanese government collapsed and fighting broke out between Christian and Islamic Lebanese in the wake of the

1982 Israeli invasion, Reagan sent American troops into Lebanon as part of an international peacekeeping force. Soon, however, Israel pulled out and the Americans came under continual shelling from the various Lebanese factions. In October 1983 a Moslem drove a truck filled with explosives into a building housing marines, killing 239. A few months later, Reagan removed all American troops from Lebanon.

8.3   ELECTION OF 1984

8.3.1   *The Democrats*

Walter Mondale, formerly a senator from Minnesota and vice president under Carter, won the Democratic nomination over Senator Gary Hart and Jesse Jackson, a black civil rights leader. Mondale chose Geraldine Ferraro, a congresswoman from New York, as his running mate. Mondale criticized Reagan for his budget deficits, high unemployment and interest rates, and reduction of spending on social services.

8.3.2   *The Reagan Victory*

The Republicans renominated Ronald Reagan and George Bush. Reagan drew support from groups such as the Moral Majority, which opposed such cultural issues as abortion and homosexual rights and advocated government aid to private schools. Reagan appealed to other voters because of his strong stand against the Soviet Union and the lowering of inflation, interest rates, and unemployment. He defeated Mondale by gaining nearly 60% of the vote, breaking apart the Democratic coalition of industrial workers, farmers, and the poor that had existed since the days of Franklin Roosevelt. Only blacks as a block continued to vote Democratic. Reagan's success did not help Republicans in Congress, however, where they lost two seats in the Senate and gained little in the House.

8.4 SECOND TERM FOREIGN CONCERNS

8.4.1 *Achille Lauro*

In October 1985 Arab terrorists seized the Italian cruise ship *Achille Lauro* in the Mediterranean, threatening to blow up the ship if 50 jailed Palestinians in Israel were not freed. They killed an elderly Jewish-American tourist and surrendered to Egyptian authorities on the condition that they be sent to Libya on an Egyptian airliner. Reagan ordered Navy F-14 jets to intercept the airliner and force it to land in Italy, where the terrorists were jailed.

8.4.2 *Libya*

Reagan challenged Muammar al-Qaddafi, the anti-American leader of Libya, by sending 6th Fleet ships within the Gulf of Sidra, which Qaddafi claimed. When Libyan gunboats challenged the American ships, American planes destroyed the gunboats and bombed installations on the Libyan shoreline. Soon after, a West German nightclub popular among American servicemen was bombed, killing a soldier and a civilian. Reagan, believing the bombing was ordered directly by Qaddafi, launched an air strike from Great Britain against Libyan bases in April 1986.

8.4.3 *Soviet Union*

After Mikhail S. Gorbachev became the premier of the Soviet Union in March 1985 and took an apparently more flexible approach toward both domestic and foreign affairs, Reagan softened his anti-Soviet stance. Nonetheless, although the Soviets said that they would continue to honor the unratified SALT II agreement, Reagan argued that they had not adhered to the pact and he sought to expand and modernize the American defense system.

8.4.4 *SDI*

Reagan concentrated on obtaining funding for the development of a computer-controlled strategic defense initiative system (SDI), popularly called "Star Wars" after the widely-seen movie, that would destroy enemy missiles from outer space. Congress balked, skeptical about the technological possibilities and fearing enormous costs.

8.4.5 *Arms Control*

SDI also appeared to prevent Reagan and Gorbachev from reaching an agreement on arms limitations at summit talks in 1985 and 1986. Finally, in December 1987, they signed an agreement eliminating medium-range missiles from Europe.

8.4.6 *Iran-Contra*

Near the end of 1986, a scandal arose involving William Casey, head of the CIA; Lieutenant Colonel Oliver North of the National Security Council; Admiral John Poindexter, national security advisor; and Robert McFarlane, former national security advisor. In 1985 and 1986, they had sold arms to the Iranians in hopes of encouraging them to use their influence in getting American hostages in Lebanon released. The profits from these sales were then diverted to the Nicaraguan contras in an attempt to get around congressional restrictions on funding the contras. The president was forced to appoint a special prosecutor and Congress held hearings on the affair in May 1987. The appeals court overturned both convictions in 1991 because congressional testimony may have influenced the proceedings; the government then dropped the cases.

8.4.7 Nicaragua

The Reagan administration did not support a peace plan signed by five Central American nations in 1987, but the following year the Sandinistas and the contras agreed on a ceasefire.

8.5 SECOND TERM DOMESTIC AFFAIRS

8.5.1 Tax Reform

The Tax Reform Act of 1986 lowered tax rates, changing the highest rate on personal income from 50% to 28% and corporate taxes from 46% to 34%. At the same time, it removed many tax shelters and tax credits. Six million low-income families did not have to pay any federal income tax at all. The law did away with the concept of progressive taxation, the requirement that the percentage of income paid as tax increased as income increased. Instead, over a two-year period it established two rates, 15% on incomes below $17,850 for individuals and $29,750 for families and 28% on incomes above these amounts. The tax system would no longer be used as an instrument of social policy.

8.5.2 Economic Patterns

Unemployment declined, reaching 6.6% in 1986, while inflation fell as low as 2.2% during the first quarter of that year. The stock market was bullish through mid-1987.

8.5.3 Oil Prices

Falling oil prices hit the Texas economy particularly hard as well as other oil-producing states of the Southwest. The oil-producing countries had to cut back on their purchases of imports, which in turn hurt all manufacturing nations. American banks suffered when oil-related international loans went unpaid.

8.5.4 *Agriculture*

During the 1970's many farmers had borrowed, because of rising prices, to expand production. Between 1975 and 1983 farm mortgages increased from under $50 billion to over $112 billion while total indebtedness increased to $215 billion. With the general slowing of inflation and the decline of world agricultural prices, many American farmers began to descend into bankruptcy in the mid-1980's, often dragging the rural banks that had made them the loans into bankruptcy as well. Although it lifted the ban on wheat exports to the Soviet Union, the Reagan administration reduced price supports and opposed debt relief passed by Congress.

8.5.5 *Deficits*

The federal deficit reached $179 billion in 1985 and about the same time the United States experienced trade deficits of more than $100 billion annually, partly because management and engineering skills had fallen behind Japan and Germany and partly because the U.S. provided an open market to foreign businesses. In the mid-1980's the United States became a debtor nation for the first time since World War I, owing more to foreigners than they owed to the U.S. Consumer debt also rose from $300 billion in 1980 to $500 billion in 1986.

8.5.6 *Mergers*

Merging of companies, encouraged by the deregulation movement of Carter and Reagan as well as the emerging international economy, and fueled by funds released by new tax breaks, became a widespread phenomenon. Twenty-seven major companies, valued from $2.6 to $13.3 billion, merged between 1981 and 1986. Multinational corporations, which produced goods in many different countries, also began to characterize the economy.

8.5.7 Black Monday

On October 19, 1987, the Dow Jones industrial average plummeted over 500 points. The stock market debacle came to be known as Black Monday. Between August 25 and October 20 the market lost over a trillion dollars in paper value. Fearing a recession, Congress in November 1987 reduced 1988 taxes by $30 billion.

8.5.8 NASA

The controversial SDI program was to be developed by the National Aeronautics and Space Administration (NASA), which had gained great prestige through its expeditions to the moon (1969–1972), Skylab orbiting space station program (1973–1974), and the space shuttle program (beginning in 1981). The explosion of the shuttle *Challenger* soon after take-off on January 28, 1986, damaged NASA's credibility and reinforced doubts about the complex technology required for the SDI program.

8.5.9 Supreme Court

Reagan considerably reshaped the Court, replacing in 1986 Chief Justice Warren C. Burger with Associate Justice William H. Rehnquist, probably the most conservative member of the Court. Although failing in his nomination of Robert Bork for associate justice, Reagan also appointed other conservatives to the Court: Sandra Day O'Connor, Antonin Scalia, and Anthony Kennedy.

8.6 ELECTION OF 1988

8.6.1 *The Democrats*

After a sex scandal eliminated Senator Gary Hart from the race for the Democratic presidential nomination, Governor Michael Dukakis of Massachusetts emerged as the victor over his major challenger Jesse Jackson. He chose Senator Lloyd Bentsen of Texas as his vice-presidential running mate.

8.6.2 *The Republicans*

Vice President George Bush, after a slow start in the primaries, won the Republican nomination. He chose Senator J. Danforth (Dan) Quayle of Indiana as his running mate.

8.6.3 *The Campaign*

After starting behind in the polls, Bush soon caught up with Dukakis by emphasizing patriotism, defense, anti-crime, and a pledge for "no new taxes." Dukakis called for competence rather than ideology but was unable to find a focus.

8.6.4 *The Election*

Bush easily defeated Dukakis, winning 40 states and 426 electoral votes, while Dukakis won only 10 states and 112 electoral votes. The Democrats gained one seat in the Senate, two seats in the House, and one governorship.

8.7 BUSH ABANDONS REAGANOMICS

8.7.1 *Budget Deficit*

Soon after George Bush took office as president on January

20, 1989, the budget deficit for 1990 was estimated at $143 billion. With deficit estimates continuing to grow, Bush held a "budget summit" with Congressional leaders in May 1990, and his administration continued talks throughout the summer. In September the administration and Congress agreed to increase taxes on gasoline, tobacco, and alcohol, establish an excise tax on luxury items, and raise medicare taxes. Cuts were also to be made in medicare and other domestic programs. The 1991 deficit was now estimated to be over $290 billion. The following month Congress approved the plan, hoping to cut a cumulative amount of $500 billion from the deficit over the next five years. In a straight party vote, Republicans voting against and Democrats voting in favor, Congress in December transferred the power to decide whether new tax and spending proposals violated the deficit-cutting agreement from the White House Office of Management and Budget to the Congressional Budget Office.

8.7.2 Defense Budget

The Commission on Base Realignment and Closure proposed in December 1989 that 54 military bases be closed. In June 1990 Secretary of Defense Richard Cheney sent to Congress a plan to cut military spending by 10% and the armed forces by 25% over the next five years. The following April, Cheney recommended the closing of 43 domestic military bases plus many more abroad.

8.7.3 Minimum Wage

In May 1989 President Bush vetoed an increase in the minimum wage from $3.35 to $4.55 an hour. But the following November, Congress approved and Bush signed an increase to $4.25 an hour, which took effect in 1991.

8.7.4 Savings and Loan Debacle

With the savings and loan industry in financial trouble in February 1989, largely because of bad real estate loans, Bush proposed to close or sell 350 institutions, to be paid for by the sale of government bonds. In July he signed a bill that created the Resolution Trust Corporation to oversee the closure and merging of S & Ls, and which provided $166 billion over 10 years to cover the bad debts. Estimates of the total cost of the debacle ran to more than $300 billion.

8.7.5 Scandals in the Financial Markets

Charges of insider trading, stock manipulation, and falsification of records resulted in Drexel Burnham Lambert, a major securities firm, pleading guilty in December 1988 to six violations of federal law. The company filed for bankruptcy and Michael Milken, its "junk bond king" (junk bonds are bonds below an investment grade of BB or Bb, but because of their risk carry a two- to three-point interest rate advantage) pleaded guilty to conspiracy, among other charges, in 1990. Meanwhile, in July 1989, 46 futures traders at the Chicago Mercantile Exchange were charged with racketeering.

8.7.6 Economic Slowdown

The Gross National Product slowed from 4.4% in 1988 to 3.6% in 1989. Unemployment gradually began to increase, reaching 7.8% in June, 1992, an eight-year high. Every sector of the economy, except for medical services, and all geographical areas experienced the slowdown. The "Big Three" automakers posted record losses and Pan American and Eastern Airlines entered into bankruptcy proceedings. The Federal Reserve cut the interest rate in 1991 and 1992 in an attempt to stimulate the economy.

8.8 OTHER DOMESTIC ISSUES UNDER THE BUSH ADMINISTRATION

8.8.1 *Exxon* Valdez

After the Exxon *Valdez* spilled more than 240,000 barrels of oil into Alaska's Prince William Sound in March 1989, the Federal Government ordered Exxon Corporation to develop a clean-up plan, which the company carried out until the weather prevented it from continuing in September. The *Valdez*'s captain, Joseph Hazelwood, was found guilty of negligence the following year. Exxon Corporation, the State of Alaska, and the U.S. Justice Department reached a settlement in October 1991 requiring Exxon to pay $1.025 billion in fines and restitution through the year 2001.

8.8.2 *Congressional Ethics Violations*

After the House Ethics Committee released a report charging that Speaker of the House Jim Wright had violated rules regulating acceptance of gifts and outside income, Wright resigned in May 1989. A short time later, the Democratic Whip Tony Coelho resigned because of alleged improper use of campaign funds. The House Bank was closed in December 1991, after revelations that it was covering personal checks of members of Congress written against insufficient funds. In 1992 the House Post Office employees were discovered to be involved in the misuse of post office funds, embezzlement, and drug dealing. Two years later, Dan Rostenkowski, Chairman of the Ways and Means Committee, was indicted on 17 felony counts, including embezzlement, fraud, and obstruction of justice. In accordance with House rules, he then resigned his chairmanship. Rostenkowski met defeat in the 1994 election.

8.8.3 Flag Burning

In May 1989 the Supreme Court ruled that the Constitution protected protesters who burned the United States flag. Bush denounced the decision and supported an amendment barring desecration of the flag. The amendment failed to pass Congress.

8.8.4 HUD Scandal

In July 1989 Secretary of Housing and Urban Development Jack Kemp revealed that the department had lost more than $2 billion under his predecessor, Samuel Pierce. A Special Prosecutor was named in February 1990 to investigate the case and the House held hearings on HUD during the next two months.

8.8.5 Medicare

In July 1988 the Medicare Catastrophic Coverage Act had placed a cap on fees Medicare patients paid to physicians and hospitals. After many senior citizens, particularly those represented by the American Association of Retired Persons (AARP), objected to the surtax that funded the program, Congress repealed the Act in November 1989.

8.8.6 Pollution

The Clean Air Act, passed in October 1990 and updating the 1970 law, mandated that the level of emissions was to be reduced 50% by the year 2000. Cleaner gasolines were to be developed, cities were to reduce ozone, and nitrogen oxide emissions were to be cut one-third.

8.8.7 Civil Rights

The Americans with Disabilities Act, passed in July 1990, barred discrimination against people with physical or mental disabilities. In October 1990 Bush vetoed the Civil Rights Act on the grounds that it established quotas, but a year later he accepted a slightly revised version that, among other things, required that employers in discrimination suits prove that their hiring practices are not discriminatory.

8.8.8 *Supreme Court Appointments*

Bush continued to reshape the Supreme Court in a conservative direction when, upon the retirement of Justice William J. Brennan, he successfully nominated Judge David Souter of the U.S. Court of Appeals in 1989. Two years later, Bush nominated a conservative Black, Judge Clarence Thomas, also of the U.S. Court of Appeals, upon the retirement of Justice Thurgood Marshall. Thomas's nomination stirred up opposition from the NAACP and other liberal groups which supported affirmative action and abortion rights. Dramatic charges of sexual harassment against Thomas from Anita Hill, a University of Oklahoma law professor, were revealed only days before the nomination was to go to the Senate, and provoked a reopening of Judiciary Committee hearings, which were nationally televised. Nonetheless, Thomas narrowly won confirmation in October 1991.

8.8.9 *Cable Regulation Bill*

After 35 successful Bush vetoes, Congress overrode the President's veto of the Cable Television Consumer Protection and Competition Act in October 1992, which gave the federal government power to regulate cable television rates.

8.9 BUSH'S ACTIVIST FOREIGN POLICY

8.9.1 *Panama*

Since coming to office, the Bush administration had been concerned with Panamanian dictator Manuel Noriega because he allegedly provided an important link in the drug traffic between South America and the United States. After economic sanctions, diplomatic efforts, and an October 1989 coup failed to oust Noriega, Bush ordered 12,000 troops into Panama on December 20. The Americans installed a new government headed by Guillermo Endara, who had earlier apparently won a presidential election which was then nullified by Noriega. Twenty-three United States soldiers and three American civilians were killed in the operation. The Panamanians lost nearly 300 soldiers and more than 500 civilians. On January 3, 1990, Noriega surrendered to the Americans and was taken to the United States to stand trial on drug trafficking charges, a trial that began in September 1991. Noriega was sentenced to forty years in prison in 1992 for racketeering, drug trafficking, and money laundering.

8.9.2 Nicaragua

After years of civil war, Nicaragua held a presidential election in February 1990. Because of an economy largely destroyed by civil war and large financial debt to the United States Violetta Barrios de Chamorro of the National Opposition Union defeated Daniel Ortega of the Sandinistas, thereby fulfilling a longstanding American objective. The United States lifted its economic sanctions in March and put together an economic aid package for Nicaragua. In September 1991, the Bush Administration forgave Nicaragua most of its debt to the United States.

8.9.3 China

After the death in April 1989 of reformer Hu Yaobang, formerly general secretary and chairman of the Chinese Communist Party, students began pro-democracy marches in Beijing. By the middle of May, more than one million people were gathering on Beijing's Tiananmen Square, and others elsewhere in China, calling for political reform. Martial law was imposed and in early June the Army fired on the demonstrators. Estimates of the death toll in the wake of the nationwide crackdown on demonstrators ranged between 500 and 7,000. In July 1989 United States National Security Advisor Brent Scowcroft and Deputy Secretary of State Lawrence Eagleburger secretly met with Chinese leaders. When they again met the Chinese, in December, and revealed their earlier meeting, the Bush administration faced a storm of criticism for its policy of "constructive engagement," by opponents arguing that sanctions were needed. Although establishing sanctions to China in 1991 on high-technology satellite-part exports, Bush continued to support renewal of China's Most Favored Nation trading status.

8.9.4 *Africa*

To rescue American citizens threatened by civil war, Bush sent 230 marines into Liberia in August 1990, evacuating 125 people. South Africa in 1990 freed Nelson Mandela, the most famous leader of the African National Congress, after 28 years of imprisonment. South Africa then began moving away from Apartheid, and in 1991 Bush lifted economic sanctions imposed five years earlier. Mandela and his wife Winnie toured the U.S. in June 1990 to a tumultuous welcome, particularly from African-Americans. During their visit, they also addressed Congress.

8.10 COLLAPSE OF EAST EUROPEAN COMMUNISM

8.10.1 *Poland*

With the Soviet Union suffering severe economic problems, and Mikhail Gorbachev stating that he would not interfere in Poland's internal affairs, Communism began to crumble in Eastern Europe. After years of effort by Solidarity, the non-Communist labor union, Poland became the first European nation to shift from Communism. Through a democratic process, Solidarity overwhelmingly won the parliamentary elections in June 1989 and Tadeuiz Mazowiecki became premier the following August.

8.10.2 Hungary

In August 1989 Hungary opened its borders with Austria. The following October, the Communists reorganized their party, calling it the Socialist party. Hungary then proclaimed itself a "Free Republic."

8.10.3 East Germany

With thousands of East Germans passing through Hungary to Austria, after the opening of the borders in August 1989, Erich Honecker stepped down as head of state in October. On November 1, the government opened the border with Czechoslovakia and eight days later the Berlin Wall fell. On December 6, a non-Communist became head of state, followed on December 11 by large demonstrations demanding German reunification. Reunification took place in October 1990.

8.10.4 Czechoslovakia

After anti-government demonstrations were forcibly broken up in Czechoslovakia in October 1989, changes took place in the Communist leadership the following month. Then, on December 8, the Communists agreed to relinquish power and Parliament elected Vaclav Havel, a playwright and anti-Communist leader, to the presidency on December 29.

8.10.5 Romania

When anti-government demonstrations were met by force in early December, portions of the military began joining the opposition, which captured dictator Nicolae Ceausescu and his wife, Elena, killing them on December 25, 1989. In May 1990, the National Salvation Front, made up of many former Communists, won the parliamentary elections.

8.10.6 *Bulgaria*

In January 1990, the Bulgarian national assembly repealed the dominant role of the Communist party. A multi-party coalition government was formed the following December.

8.10.7 *Albania*

Albania opened its border with Greece and legalized religious worship in January 1990, and in July ousted hard-liners from the government.

8.10.8 *Bush-Gorbachev Summits*

Amid the collapse of Communism in Eastern Europe, Bush met with Mikhail Gorbachev in Malta from December 1 through 3, 1989; the two leaders appeared to agree that the Cold War was over. On May 30–31, 1990, Bush and Gorbachev met in Washington to discuss the possible reunification of Germany, and signed a trade treaty between the United States and the Soviet Union. The meeting of the two leaders in Helsinki on September 9 addressed strategies for the developing Persian Gulf crisis. At the meeting of the "Group of 7" nations (Canada, France, Germany, Italy, Japan, United Kingdom, and the United States) in July 1991, Gorbachev requested economic aid from the West. A short time later, on July 30 and 31, Bush met Gorbachev in Moscow where they signed the START treaty. The accord cut U.S. and Soviet nuclear arsenals by 30%, and pushed for Middle Eastern talks.

8.11 PERSIAN GULF CRISIS

8.11.1 *July 1990*

Saddam Hussein of Iraq charged that Kuwait had conspired with the United States to keep oil prices low and began massing troops at the Iraq-Kuwait border.

8.11.2 *August 1990*

On August 2, Iraq invaded Kuwait, an act that Bush denounced as "naked aggression." One day later 100,000 Iraqi soldiers were poised south of Kuwait City near the Saudi Arabian border. The United States quickly banned most trade with Iraq, froze Iraq's and Kuwait's assets in the United States, and sent aircraft carriers to the Persian Gulf. After the United Nations Security Council condemned the invasion, on August 6 Bush ordered the deployment of air, sea, and land forces to Saudi Arabia, dubbing the operation "Desert Shield." At the end of August there were 100,000 American soldiers in Saudi Arabia.

8.11.3 *September 1990*

Bush encouraged Egypt to support American policy by forgiving Egypt its debt to the United States and obtaining pledges of financial support from Saudi Arabia, Kuwait, and Japan, among other nations, to help pay for the operation.

8.11.4 *October 1990*

On October 29, the Security Council warned Hussein that further actions might be taken if he did not withdraw from Kuwait.

8.11.5 November 1990

In November, Bush ordered that U.S. forces be increased to more than 400,000. On November 29, the United Nations set January 15, 1991, as the deadline for Iraqi withdrawal from Kuwait.

8.11.6 January 1991

On January 9, Iraq's foreign-minister, Tariq Aziz, rejected a letter written by Bush to Hussein. Three days later, after an extensive debate, Congress authorized the use of force in the Gulf. On January 17, an international force including the United States, Great Britain, France, Italy, Saudi Arabia, and Kuwait launched an air and missile attack on Iraq and occupied Kuwait. The U.S. called the effort "Operation Desert Storm." Under the overall command of Army General H. Norman Schwarzkopf, the military effort emphasized high-technology weapons, including F-15 E fighter-bombers, F-117 A stealth fighters, Tomahawk cruise missiles, and Patriot anti-missile missiles. Beginning on January 17, Iraq sent SCUD missiles into Israel in an effort to draw that country into the war and hopefully break up the U.S.-Arabian coalition. On January 22 and 23, Hussein's forces set Kuwaiti oil fields on fire and spilled oil into the Gulf.

8.11.7 February 1991

On February 23, the allied ground assault began. Four days later Bush announced that Kuwait was liberated and ordered offensive operations to cease. The United Nations established the terms for the cease fire: Iraqi annexation of Kuwait to be rescinded, Iraq to accept liability for damages and return Kuwaiti property, Iraq to end all military actions and identify mines and booby traps, and Iraq to release captives.

8.11.8 *April 1991*

On April 3, the Security Council approved a resolution to establish a permanent cease-fire; Iraq accepted U.N. terms on April 6. The next day the United States began airlifting food to Kurdish refugees on the Iraq-Turkey border who were fleeing the Kurdish rebellion against Hussein, a rebellion that was seemingly encouraged by Bush who nonetheless refused to become militarily involved. The United States estimated that 100,000 Iraqis had been killed during the war while the Americans had lost about 115 lives.

8.11.9 *Toward a Middle East Peace Conference*

On February 6, 1991, the United States had set out its postwar goals for the Middle East. These included regional arms control and security arrangements, international aid for reconstruction of Iraq and Kuwait, and resolution of the Israeli-Palestinian conflict. Immediately after cessation of the conflict, Secretary of State James Baker toured the Middle East attempting to promote a conference to address the problems of the region. After several more negotiating sessions, Saudi Arabia, Syria, Jordan, and Lebanon had accepted the United States proposal for an Arab-Israeli peace conference by the middle of July; Israel conditionally accepted in early August. Despite continuing conflict with Iraq, including United Nations inspections of its nuclear capabilities, and new Israeli settlements in disputed territory which kept the conference agreement tenuous, the nations met in Madrid, Spain at the end of October. Bilateral talks in early November between Israel and the Arabs concentrated on procedural issues.

8.12   BREAKUP OF THE SOVIET UNION

8.12.1 *Lithuania*

Following the collapse of Communism in Eastern Europe, the Baltic republic of Lithuania, which had been taken over by the Soviet Union in 1939 owing to an agreement with Adolph Hitler, declared its independence from the Soviet Union on March 11, 1990.

8.12.2 *Soviet Liberalization*

Two days later, on March 13, the Soviet Union removed the Communist monopoly of political power, allowing non-Communists to run for office. The process of liberalization went haltingly forward in the Soviet Union. Perhaps the most significant event was the election of Boris Yeltsin, who had left the Communist party, as president of the Russian republic on June 12, 1991. (Eight and a half years later, on New Year's Eve 1999, an ailing Yeltsin, in a surprise announcement, would resign.)

8.12.3 *Soviet Coup Attempt*

On August 19, Soviet hard-liners attempted a coup to oust Gorbachev, but a combination of their inability to control communication with the outside world, a failure to quickly establish military control, and the resistance of Yeltsin, members of the military, and people in the streets of cities such as Moscow and Leningrad ended the coup on August 21, returning Gorbachev to power.

8.12.4 *Collapse of Soviet Communism*

In the aftermath of the August 1991 coup attempt, much of the Soviet Communist structure came crashing down, and the

Communist Party itself was prohibited. The remaining Baltic republics of Latvia and Estonia declared their independence, which was recognized by the United States several days after other nations had done so. Most of the other Soviet republics then followed suit in declaring their independence. The Bush administration wanted some form of central authority to remain in the Soviet Union; hence, it did not seriously consider recognizing the independence of any republics except the Baltics. In December 1991, however, the Soviet Union disbanded and was replaced by the loosely organized Commonwealth of Independent States.

8.12.5 *Arms Reduction*

In September 1991 President Bush announced unilateral removal and destruction of ground-based tactical nuclear weapons in Europe and Asia, removal of nuclear-armed Tomahawk cruise missiles from surface ships and submarines, immediate destruction of intercontinental ballistic missiles covered by START, and an end to the round-the-clock alert for strategic bombers that the U.S. had maintained for decades. Gorbachev responded the next month by announcing the immediate deactivation of intercontinental ballistic missiles covered by START, removal of all short-range missiles from Soviet ships, submarines, and aircraft, and destruction of all ground-based tactical nuclear weapons. He also said that the Soviet Union would reduce its forces by 700,000 troops, and he placed all long-range nuclear missiles under a single command. In January 1993 Bush and Yeltsin signed START II, under which the two sides agreed to cut warheads by two-thirds, from about 10,000 each to 3,500 for the U.S. and 3,000 for Russia by 2003.

8.13 SOCIAL AND CULTURAL DEVELOPMENTS

8.13.1 *AIDS*

In 1981 scientists announced the discovery of Acquired Immune Deficiency Syndrome (AIDS), which was especially widespread among homosexual males and intravenous drug users. Widespread fear resulted, including an upsurge in homophobia. The Centers for Disease Control and Prevention and the National Cancer Institute, among others, pursued research on the disease. By 1990, 600,000 Americans had the virus, 83,000 had died, and another 136,000 were sick. The FDA responded to calls for faster evaluation of drugs by approving the drug AZT in February 1991. With the revelation that a Florida dentist had infected three patients, there were calls for mandatory testing of health care workers. Supporters of testing argued before a House hearing in September 1991 that testing should be regarded as a public health issue, rather than a civil rights issue.

8.13.2 *Religious Right*

In 1987 it was revealed that popular TV preacher Jim Bakker had been involved in a sex and money scandal. A short time later, one of his major critics, evangelist Jimmy Swaggart, was discovered to be in a sex scandal of his own. With the influence of TV evangelists on the wane, Jerry Falwell announced that he was abandoning political activism to concentrate on preaching. In October 1991 Jim Bakker was convicted of fraud and conspiracy.

8.13.3 *Families*

More than half the married women in the United States continued to hold jobs outside the home. More than a million marriages ended in divorce annually and there was an increase in the number of couples living together without getting married, which contributed to the growing number of illegitimate births. Abortions increased from 763,000 in 1974, the year following *Roe v. Wade*, to 1.3 million in 1981.

8.13.4 *Crime and Drugs*

The number of prisoners reached 464,000, a record number, in 1985. Drugs continued to be used widely, with cocaine becoming more readily available, particularly in a cheaper and stronger form called "crack." In 1989 Bush declared a "war on drugs" and appointed William Bennett to coordinate national drug control policy. The following year Bush met with presidents of Bolivia, Colombia, and Peru, and signed an anti-drug agreement. Robert Martinez replaced Bennett in 1991.

8.13.5 *Labor*

Labor union membership dropped to about 19% of the labor force, largely because the economy was shifting from heavy industry to electronics and service industries.

8.13.6 *Abortion*

In a July 1989 decision, *Webster v. Reproductive Health Services,* the Supreme Court upheld a Missouri law prohibiting public employees from performing abortions, unless the mother's life was threatened. With this decision shifting the abortion focus from the courts to the state legislatures, pro-life (anti-abortion) forces moved in several states to restrict the availability of abortions, but their results were mixed. Florida rejected abortion restrictions in October 1989, the governor of Louisiana vetoed similar legislation nine months later, and in early 1991 Maryland adopted a liberal abortion law. In contrast, Utah and Pennsylvania enacted strict curbs on abortion during the same period. At the national level, Bush in October 1989 vetoed funding for medicaid abortions. The conflict between pro-choice (pro-abortion) and pro-life forces gained national attention through such events as a pro-life demonstration held in Washington in April 1990, and blockage of access to abortion clinics by Operation Rescue, a militant anti-abortion group, in the summer of 1991.

8.13.7 *Rich and Poor*

Kevin Phillips's *The Politics of Rich and Poor* (1990) argued that 40 million Americans in the bottom fifth of the population experienced a 1% decline in income between 1973 and 1979 and a 10% decline between 1979 and 1987. Meanwhile, the top fifth rose by 7% and 16% during the same periods. The number of single-parent families living below the poverty level of $11,611 for a family of four rose by 46% between 1979 and 1987. Nearly one-quarter of the children under age six were poor. In 1992 14.5% of Americans were living below the poverty level, the highest since 1964. The average median family income declined for the second straight year.

8.13.8 *Censorship*

The conservative leaning of the electorate for the past decade revealed its cultural dimension in a controversy that erupted over the National Endowment for the Arts in September 1989. Criticism of photographer Robert Mapplethorpe's homoerotic and masochistic pictures, among other artworks which had been funded by the Endowment, led Senator Jesse Helms of North Carolina to propose that grants for "obscene or indecent" projects, or those derogatory of religion, be cut off. Although the proposal ultimately failed, it raised questions of the government's role as a sponsor of art in an increasingly pluralistic society. The Mapplethorpe photographs also became an issue the following summer when Cincinnati's Contemporary Art Center was indicted on charges of obscenity when it exhibited the artist's work. A jury later struck down the charges. Meanwhile, in March 1990 the Recording Industry Association of America agreed to place new uniform warning labels on recordings that contained potentially offensive language. The issue of language was dramatized when a federal judge in Florida ruled in June 1990 that the 2 Live Crew album, *As Nasty as They Wanna Be,* was obscene. A few days later two of the band members and a record store owner were arrested for violating state obscenity laws. Civil liberties groups protested. The band members were later acquitted while the businessman was convicted.

8.13.9 *Los Angeles Riots*

The 1991 videotaped beating of Rodney King by Los Angeles police officers resulted in a trial which acquitted the police in April 1992. Violence erupted in South-Central Los Angeles, lasting from April 29 to May 1 and resulting in fifty-two deaths, 600 buildings destroyed, and over one billion dollars in damages. Army, Marine, and National Guard units were called in to stop the riot. Two of the police officers were convicted in 1993 in federal court of violating King's civil rights.

8.13.10 *Tailhook Scandal*

A 1991 convention of the Tailhook Association of Navy and Marine fliers produced complaints of sexual harassment. An investigation revealed that 26 women had been abused. In 1994 Chief of Naval Operations, Frank B. Kelso II, took early retirement after being accused of manipulating the investigation.

8.13.11 *Crisis in Education*

The National Commission on Excellence in Education, appointed in 1981, argued in "A Nation at Risk" that the nation's schools were caught in a "rising tide of mediocrity." In the wake of the report many states instituted reforms, including higher teacher salaries, competency tests for teachers, and an increase in required subjects for high school graduation. In

September 1989, Bush met with the nation's governors in Charlottesville, Virginia, to craft a plan to improve the public schools. In February 1990, the National Governors Association adopted specific performance goals, calling for achievement tests to be administered in grades four, eight, and twelve. (As the new millennium approached, tentative signs began to emerge that the tide might be turning: a major global comparison in June 1997 found that America's 9- and 10-year-olds were among the world's best in science and also scored well above average in math. Education continued to be a flashpoint in political debate on the local and national levels. A major vein of reform was opened up with the establishment of charter schools— autonomous public schools—which were given their autonomy and were deregulated in exchange for time limits being placed on their charters, or contracts, for student achievement. Charter terms typically ran for five years or so. On the principle of per-pupil allotment, public monies flowed to these schools.)

8.13.12 *Literary Trends*

Though not a major literary decade, the 1980's saw the emergence of writers who concentrated on marginal aspects of national life. William Kennedy wrote a series of novels about Albany, New York, most notably *Ironweed* (1983). The small-town West attracted attention from Larry McMurtry, whose *Lonesome Dove* (1985) used myth to explore the history of the region. The immigrant experience gave rise to Amy Tan's *The Joy-Luck Club* (1989) and Oscar Hijuelos's *The Mambo Kings Play Songs of Love* (1990). Tom Wolfe satirized greed, and class and racial tensions in New York City in *The Bonfire of the Vanities* (1987). John Updike's *Rabbit at Rest* (1990) closed out his quartet of novels examining middle-class life.

8.13.13 *Film*

Steven Spielberg began his Indiana Jones series with *Raiders of the Lost Ark* (1981). The social concerns that roiled 1960's America came to the silver screen in *The Big Chill* (1983), *Platoon* (1986), and *Born on the Fourth of July* (1989). Intergenerational conflict and bonding was featured in *On Golden Pond* (1981), while *Driving Miss Daisy* (1989) examined race relations.

8.13 .14 *Theater*

Notable plays included Harvey Fierstein's *Torch Song Trilogy* (1983), August Wilson's *Fences* (1987), David Henry Hwang's *M. Butterfly* (1988), and Wendy Wasserstein's *The Heidi Chronicles* (1989).

8.14 ELECTION OF 1992

8.14.1 *The Democrats*

William Jefferson Clinton, governor of Arkansas, emerged from a crowded field in the primaries to win the Democratic nomination. He chose Senator Albert Gore of Tennessee as his vice presidential running mate.

8.14.2 *The Republicans*

President George Bush and Vice President J. Danforth (Dan) Quayle easily won the Republican nomination, despite a challenge from conservative columnist Patrick Buchanan.

8.14.3 *Ross Perot*

Texas entrepreneur H. Ross Perot entered the campaign as an independent, making effective use of television and pledging to reduce the deficit and make government work.

8.14.4 *The Campaign*

Clinton and Perot emphasized the economy, particularly the

deficit and the need to create more jobs. Bush called for a return to "traditional values" and publicized his foreign policy achievements.

8.14.5 The Election

Clinton won 43% (44,909,889) of the popular vote and 370 electoral votes while Bush gained 37% (39,104,545) of the popular vote and 168 electoral votes. Although he won no electoral votes, Perot achieved 19% (19,742,267) of the popular vote.

CHAPTER 9

THE CLINTON PRESIDENCY, 1993–2001

9.1 DOMESTIC AFFAIRS

9.1.1 *Homosexuality in the Military*

President Bill Clinton created a storm of controversy in January 1993 when he proposed lifting the ban on gays and lesbians in the military. In July 1993, a compromise "Don't ask, don't tell" policy was adopted, requiring gays and lesbians to be discreet about their sexual orientation and not to engage in homosexual acts.

9.1.2 *Abortion*

In January 1993 Clinton lifted restrictions on abortion established by the Bush administration, including the "gag rule" forbidding discussion of abortion with patients at federally funded family planning clinics and the ban on use of fetal tissue for research. In 1993 and 1994 abortion rights opponents killed two abortion doctors in Pensacola, Florida.

9.1.3 Family and Medical Leave Act

Vetoed earlier by Bush, the Family and Medical Leave Bill, which Clinton signed in February 1993, required large companies to provide up to 12 weeks' unpaid leave for family and medical emergencies.

9.1.4 World Trade Center Bombing

While terrorist attacks continued to be a grim reality overseas through the 1980's and early 1990's—with Americans frequently targeted—such incidents had come to be perceived as something the United States wouldn't have to face on its own soil—until February 26, 1993, when a terrorist bomb ripped through the underground parking garage of the World Trade Center in New York City, killing six people and injuring more than 1,000. The blast shattered America's "myth of invulnerability," wrote foreign policy analyst Jeffrey D. Simon in his book *The Terrorist Trap*. Convicted and sentenced to 240 years each were four Islamic militants.

9.1.5 "Motor-Voter" Bill

Passed in 1993, the "Motor-Voter" bill required states to allow citizens to register to vote while applying for driver's licenses and to adopt standardized procedures for voter-registration by mail.

9.1.6 Branch Davidians

In February 1993 the U.S. Bureau of Alcohol, Tobacco, and Firearms raided the headquarters of the Branch Davidian religious cult near Waco, Texas, resulting in four federal agents being killed. After a 51-day standoff, from February 28 to April 26, the FBI attacked the compound with tear gas and began destroying walls of the compound. Cult members apparently started a fire, resulting in the deaths of 72 Branch Davidians, including their leader David Koresh.

9.1.7 Budget Deficit

The Omnibus Budget Reconciliation Act of 1993 sought to reduce the federal deficit by $496 billion by 1998. It combined $225 billion in spending cuts with $241 billion in new taxes over five years. The tax increases affected incomes over $115,000.

9.1.8 National Service

The 1993 National Service bill allowed a limited number of young people to repay federal education assistance through community service.

9.1.9 Natural Disasters

Floods struck states from South Dakota to Missouri in the summer of 1993, covering 16 million acres and causing more than $10 billion in damages, and 50 deaths. In January 1994 an earthquake hit Los Angeles, killing 51 people and causing between $15 and $30 billion in damage.

9.1.10 NAFTA

The North American Free Trade Agreement, negotiated by the Bush administration, eliminated most tariffs and other trade barriers between the United States, Canada, and Mexico. Passed by Congress in 1993, it went into effect in January 1994. Opposed strongly by organized labor and Ross Perot, Clinton pushed the bill through Congress with Republican support.

9.1.11 Gun Control

The Brady Handgun Violence Prevention Act, adopted in 1993, established a five-day waiting period for the purchase of handguns to enable local law-enforcement officials to check the background of prospective buyers.

9.1.12 *Economy*

As of February 1, 2000, the U.S. economy had enjoyed the longest stretch of uninterrupted growth in the nation's history; the expansion had begun in March 1991. Unemployment and inflation were both notably low.

9.1.13 *Labor*

Labor union strength continued to ebb in the 1990's, with the U.S. Department of Labor's Bureau of Labor Statistics reporting that union membership as a percent of wage and salary employment dropped to 14.5 percent in 1996, down from 14.9 percent in 1995. In 1983, union members made up 20.1 percent of the work force. Unions continued to be responsible for higher wages for their members: organized workers reported median weekly earnings of $615, as against a median of $462 for non-union workers, according to the bureau. (The Teamsters' strike against United Parcel Service in the summer of 1997 was seen as possibly signalling renewed strength in the union movement as a whole.)

9.1.14 *Crime Bill*

Adopted in 1994 the crime bill authorized spending $13.45 billion for state, local, and federal police, with an emphasis on community policing, $9.85 billion for prisons, and $6.9 billion for crime prevention programs. It also banned 19 types of assault weapons, imposed life sentences for third-time violent felons and drug offenders convicted in federal courts, and created over 50 new federal death penalty crimes.

9.1.15 *Supreme Court*

Clinton appointed moderates Ruth Bader Ginsburg (1993) and Stephen Breyer (1994) as Associate Justices of the Supreme Court.

9.1.16 *Health Care Reform*

In October 1993, the Clinton administration proposed legislation to reform the health care system which included universal coverage with a guaranteed benefits package, managed competition through health care alliances which would bargain with insurance companies, and employer mandates to provide health insurance for employees. Opposed by most Republicans, small business, and insurance and medical-business interests, Senate Majority Leader George Mitchell dropped his attempt at compromise legislation in September 1994.

9.1.17 *Whitewater Scandal*

Clinton was criticized for alleged wrongdoing in connection with the Whitewater real estate development in Arkansas, in which he had been an investor with James B. and Susan McDougal, co-owners of a failed savings and loan institution, while serving as the state's governor. Though the term *Whitewater* originally applied only to a land deal, it grew over time to embrace a labyrinthine series of questionable transactions at whose heart lay a number of loans allegedly doled out to well-placed Arkansans without the benefit of standard applications, down payments, or the like. The Justice Department appointed Robert B. Fiske "special counsel" to investigate the land deal in January 1994. After Congress renewed the independent counsel law, a three-judge panel appointed Kenneth W. Starr to replace Fiske. (Following the Starr investigation, Congress had a change of heart and allowed the law to expire in mid-1999.)

9.1.18 *1994 Midterm Elections*

The American people expressed apparent dissatisfaction with President Clinton, big government, taxes, and social problems such as crime by giving Republicans, most of whom were conservative, control of both houses of Congress. It was the first time since 1952 that they had won a majority in the House of Representatives. The South, once a Democratic stronghold, was now clearly moving into the Republican camp. On the state level, Republicans dominated the gubernatorial races.

9.1.19 O.J. Simpson Murder Trial

In Los Angeles, former pro-football star, broadcaster, and actor O.J. Simpson was tried for the brutal murder in June 1994 of his ex-wife, Nicole Brown Simpson, and her friend Ronald Goldman. The nationally televised trial became a running spectacle for months, with the lengthy, tortuous courtroom proceedings transfixing the nation. Simpson was found not guilty, but would later, in a civil trial, be found responsible for the slaying of Goldman and for committing battery against Nicole. The civil judgment awarded the plaintiffs, Ronald's parents and Nicole's estate, $33.5 million in damages.

9.1.20 Oklahoma City Bombing

On April 19, 1995, in the deadliest act of domestic terrorism in U.S. history, the Alfred P. Murrah federal building in Oklahoma City was bombed: 168 people were killed and 500 injured. Timothy James McVeigh, a gun enthusiast involved in the American militia movement who had often expressed hatred toward the U.S. federal government and was particularly aggrieved over the government's assault exactly two years earlier on a self-proclaimed prophet's compound in Waco, Texas, was convicted and sentenced to death in June 1997. A second defendant, Terry Nichols, was convicted on conspiracy charges.

9.2 FOREIGN POLICY

9.2.1 Somalia

In May 1993 the United Nations took control of relief efforts in Somalia from United States troops. The last U.S. soldiers left in 1994.

9.2.2 Middle East

Itzhak Rabin, Prime Minister of Israel, and Yasir Arafat, Chairman of the Palestine Liberation Organization, signed an accord in 1994 establishing Palestinian self-rule in the Gaza Strip and Jericho. The PLO began establishing control over its territory in the summer of 1994. In October 1994 Israel and Jordan signed a treaty to begin the process of establishing full diplomatic relations.

9.2.3 *Haiti*

In an attempt to force the ouster of the military government that had overthrown the democratically elected Jean-Bertrand Aristide in 1991, the Clinton administration succeeded in pushing the United Nations to establish an oil and arms embargo against Haiti in 1993. The embargo was extended the following year to include virtually everything except food and medicine. The United States banned all commercial flights to Haiti in 1994. Refugees from Haiti into the United States continued to be a major problem for the administration, which refused to let most of them enter the country. In September, after threats that an invasion was imminent, Lt. General Raoul Cedras and the remainder of the military junta agreed to relinquish power. The U.S. then led a multinational force that entered the island to ensure social stability during the period of transition; Aristide resumed the presidency in October.

9.2.4 *Korea*

North Korea threatened in 1993 to withdraw from the Nuclear Nonproliferation Treaty which led to several months of tensions over international inspection of its nuclear sites. Diplomatic discussions between North Korea and the United States, although delayed by the death of North Korean leader Kim Il Sung in July, 1994, led to an agreement which included American financial and technological assistance for North Korean nuclear energy. In return, North Korea accepted the Nuclear Nonproliferation Treaty.

9.2.5 NATO

In 1994 the North Atlantic Treaty Organization offered former members of the Warsaw Pact limited association to enhance European security.

9.2.6 *Vietnam*

The Clinton administration in 1994 lifted the trade embargo against Vietnam because of its cooperation with efforts to find the remains of U.S. military personnel.

9.2.7 *China*

In 1994 China's "Most Favored Nation" status was continued, despite Clinton's previous statements regarding the lack of improvements in political freedom in that country.

9.2.8 *Cuba*

As thousands of Cuban refugees began coming to the United States in August 1994, the Clinton administration ended their admittance to the country and began placing all refugees at the U.S. military base at Guantanamo Bay, Cuba. An agreement was reached with Cuba in September 1994 to allow 20,000 Cuban immigrants into the United States annually. The Cuban government, in return, would seek to prevent its citizens from leaving Cuba in rafts and other boats for illegal entry into the United States.

9.2.9 *Iraq*

On October 7, 1994, in response to an Iraqi military buildup on its border with Kuwait, Clinton ordered American troops, ships, and aircraft to the region and demanded that Saddam Hussein pull his forces back from the border. Four days later, the Iraqi troops began withdrawing. Hussein apparently had been hoping to force the United Nations to lift its sanctions against his country.

9.3 ELECTION OF 1996

9.3.1 *Clinton's Re-election*

Clinton recaptured the Democratic nomination without a serious challenge. Meanwhile, longtime GOP Senator Robert Dole of Kansas, the Senate majority leader, had to overcome several opponents, but orchestrated a harmonious nominating convention with running mate Jack Kemp, a former New York congressman and Cabinet member in the Bush administration. In November 1996, with most voters citing a healthy economy and the lack of an enticing alternative in Dole or the Reform Party's Perot, Clinton received 49 percent of the vote, becoming the first Democrat to be re-elected since FDR, in 1936. The GOP retained control of both houses of Congress.

9.4 IMPEACHMENT OF THE PRESIDENT

9.4.1 *Congress's Reaction to the Starr Report*

Independent Counsel Starr's investigation into alleged Clinton misdeeds yielded massive findings in late 1998, roughly midway into the president's second term, but they were far afield of Whitewater or any of the several other matters that Starr had said he'd been looking into. Instead, the Starr Report focused on an adulterous affair that Clinton had had with Monica S. Lewinsky, a White House intern. It was on charges stemming from this report that the president was impeached by the House of Representatives in December 1998. The Senate acquitted him in February 1999. The vote was overwhelmingly along party lines.

9.5 SOCIETY AND CULTURE

9.5.1 *Literature*

Spiritual concerns appeared in Anne Tyler's *Saint Maybe* (1991). In 1993 Toni Morrison became the first black woman to win the Nobel Prize for literature. Her novels, which explored the African-American experience, included *Song of Solomon* (1977), *Beloved* (1987), and *Jazz* (1992).

9.5.2 *Film*

Revisionist views of history became popular, particularly through Kevin Costner's *Dances with Wolves* (1990), Oliver Stone's *JFK* (1991), and Spike Lee's *Malcolm X* (1992). Steven Spielberg provided thrills with *Jurassic Park* (1993) and ethical reflection with *Schindler's List* (1993). Disney continued its long tradition of successful animated films with *Beauty and the Beast* (1991), *Aladdin* (1992), *The Lion King* (1994), and, of course, *Harry Potter and the Sorcerer's Stone* and its sequel (2001, 2002), which were adapted from the J.K. Rowling books.

9.5.3 *Religion*

Evidence emerged that the membership decline of the mainline churches had bottomed out, while the growth rate of conservative churches was slowing. (Church- and synagogue-going is notoriously difficult to measure, as Americans display a propensity to say they're in the pews more than they actually are: Estimates in the late 1990s of the percentage of adult Americans who claimed to have attended weekly services during the past week consistently hovered around the 40% mark; however, studies in both the U.S. and Canada have shown self-reported attendance to be widely inflated.) Roman Catholicism continued to be racked by such issues as women in the priesthood, celibacy of priests, and birth control and abortion. A visit to the United States in 1993 by Pope John Paul, who reaffirmed Catholic tradition, did not settle matters. A widening minority of Americans pursued the variety of Western and Eastern religious and occult practices and beliefs popularly lumped under the heading "New Age." Meanwhile, a rabbinical group representing the Orthodox, or ultratraditional, wing of American Judaism issued a controversial statement in 1997 that drew howls of protest from within the Jewish community by seeming to read Conservative and Reform Jews out of the mainstream. Rabbis and other Jewish leaders subsequently worked to assuage their differences. (In general, Conservative and Reform Jews seek to incorporate ideas of modernity in their observance; Orthodox Jews tend to view many such notions as concessions to the non-Jewish world.)

9.5.4 Health Issues

Beginning in 1990, Dr. Jack Kevorkian of Michigan raised the issue of assisted suicide by helping patients who were described as terminally ill end their lives. He would later bring consideration of the issue of euthanasia to a head by directly challenging prosecutors to act by giving CBS News the opportunity to show a Kevorkian-assisted suicide on the network's "60 Minutes" newsmagazine. The airing of the video led to Dr. Kevorkian's conviction in March 1999 on second-degree murder charges for helping a man with ALS, or Lou Gehrig's disease, to die. In January 1992 the Food and Drug Administration halted the sale and implantation of silicone-gel breast implants after questions of their safety arose. In 1994 eight medical supply companies agreed to pay into a fund totaling $4.2 billion to compensate women who suffered complications from these implants. Responding to growing concern over the negative effects of dietary fat, food manufacturers, under orders from the FDA, began in May 1994 to use new labeling on their packaged foods which gave the percentage of daily recommended amounts per serving for various substances, including fats.

9.5.4.1 AIDS: Victims' Complexion Changes

The Centers for Disease Control and Prevention reported in 1998 that between 400,000 and 650,000 Americans were HIV-positive, meaning that they had the virus that causes AIDS. Public health officials expressed concern about the difficulties in tracking the spread of AIDS, as the HIV infection was being reported to health agencies only when patients developed symptoms, which could be years after infection. New drug therapies, meanwhile, were preventing AIDS symptoms from ever appearing, creating the specter of growing numbers of people going unseen by public-health agencies as they spread the virus. There was also a marked change in the demographic makeup of the epidemic's victims—from mostly white homosexual males to African Americans, Hispanics, and women, particularly those who were poor, intravenous drug users, or the sex partners of drug users.

9.5.5 *The Election of 2000*

The Democrats nominated Vice President Al Gore for president and Senator Joseph Lieberman for vice president. The Republican Party nominated Texas Governor George W. Bush (son of President George Bush). After some conflict, the Reform party nominated Patrick Buchanan. The Green party ran Ralph Nader. After one of the tightest presidential elections ever, highlighted by a withdrawn concession by Gore, a recount in Florida, and several court challenges, Bush was declared the winner by the U.S. Supreme Court.

9.5.6 *The U.S. Counts Its People*

The 2000 decennial census counted 281,421,906 Americans, a 13.2% increase since 1990. The most populous state was California (33,871,648), the least populous, Wyoming (493,782).

9.5.7 *Terrorism Hits Home*

Major symbols of U.S. economic and military might—the World Trade Center in New York and the Pentagon just outside Washington, D.C.—were attacked on September 11, 2001, when hijackers deliberately crashed commercial jetliners into the buildings, causing the toppling of the trade center's 110-story twin towers. Another hijacked plane, now believed to have had the White House as its target, crashed into the ground in southwestern Pennsylvania after passengers locked in a heroic struggle with the terrorists. Thousands died in the worst act of terrorism in American history. The prime suspect, said President Bush, was Saudi exile Osama bin Laden, the alleged mastermind of previous attacks on U.S. interests abroad. Terrorist attacks had continued to be a grim reality overseas through the 1980s and early 1990s, with Americans frequently targeted. Yet such incidents had come to be viewed as something the United States wouldn't have to face on its own soil—until February 26, 1993, when a terrorist bomb ripped through the underground parking garage of the World Trade Center in New York City, killing six people and injuring more than 1,000. Convicted and sentenced to 240 years each were four Islamic militants. On April 19, 1995, the Oklahoma City federal building was bombed, killing 168 people and injuring 500. Timothy James McVeigh, a member of the American militia movement who had expressed hatred toward the U.S. government and was aggrieved over its assault two years earlier on a self-proclaimed prophet's compound in Waco, Texas, was put to death for the crime in June 2001. A second defendant, Terry Nichols, was convicted on federal charges of conspiracy and involuntary manslaughter and sentenced to life in prison.

9.5.8 The Iraq War

Claiming that Saddam Hussein harbored weapons of mass destruction (WMDs) and was connected with al Qaeda, the George W. Bush administration launched a preemptive war against Iraq on March 20, 2003. Although about thirty nations joined what was often referred to as the "coalition forces," only the United States and Great Britain contributed substantial numbers of soldiers. Initial military victory was swift, with the Hussein regime falling by April 9; Bush declared an end to major combat operations on May 1. The military was unable to find the WMDs, however, and it was ultimately concluded that prewar intelligence had been wrong. Despite the apparent victory of the coalition forces, armed opposition appeared almost immediately. Using such methods as traditional warfare, suicide bombings, remote-controlled bombs, and kidnappings, the insurgents were particularly strong in the "Sunni Triangle," an area roughly defined as a triangle with points at Baghdad (to the east), Tikrit (to the north), and Ramadi (to the west). The city of Fallujah became a resistance stronghold under the leadership of Abu Musab al-Zarqawi, a Jordanian, until American forces drove the rebels out in November 2004. Meanwhile, the Bush administration's decision to go to war and its handling of the conflict became an issue in the 2004 presidential election.

9.5.9   *The Presidential Election of 2004*

After a series of primary victories, Senator John F. Kerry of Massachusetts won the Democratic nomination for president and chose a former rival, Senator John R. Edwards of South Carolina, as his vice presidential running mate. The Republicans renewed their nomination of President George W. Bush and Vice President Richard B. Cheney. Kerry challenged Bush's economic policy and his handling of the Iraq War. In turn, Bush described Kerry as a liberal who favored high taxes and as a "flip-flopper" who could not be trusted with the nation's security; Bush presented himself, in contrast, as one who would provide firm leadership against terrorism. As in 2000, Ralph Nader ran a third party campaign, but had little effect on the election's outcome. Bush won the popular vote with 51 percent (to Kerry's 48 percent). He carried all states except those on the Pacific Coast, in the upper Midwest, and in the Northeast, thereby gaining 286 electoral votes to Kerry's 252. Republicans increased their control of both houses of Congress (they had regained the Senate in 2002). Although international issues dominated the campaign, exit polls suggested that moral values played a significant role among those who supported George W. Bush, many of whom described themselves as evangelical Christians. Not surprisingly, referendums opposing gay marriages, which had emerged as an issue partly because of recent judicial decisions, passed in all eleven states where they appeared on the ballot.

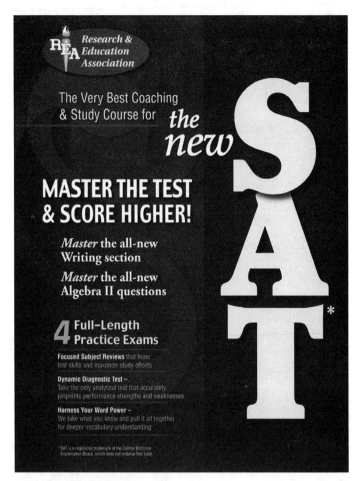

"The ESSENTIALS" of HISTORY

REA's **Essentials of History** series offers a new approach to the study of history that is different from what has been available previously. Compared with conventional history outlines, the **Essentials of History** offer far more detail, with fuller explanations and interpretations of historical events and developments. Compared with voluminous historical tomes and textbooks, the **Essentials of History** offer a far more concise, less ponderous overview of each of the periods they cover.

The **Essentials of History** provide quick access to needed information, and will serve as handy reference sources at all times. The **Essentials of History** are prepared with REA's customary concern for high professional quality and student needs.

If you would like more information about any of these books,
complete the coupon below and return it to us or visit your local bookstore.